SAN RAMON

D0577078

T H E

FARMHOUSE

AMERICAN DESIGN

THE FARMHOUSE

TEXT BY CHIPPY IRVINE, DES. R.C.A.
PHOTOGRAPHS BY DENNIS KRUKOWSKI
FOREWORD BY J. JACKSON WALTER,
PRESIDENT, THE NATIONAL TRUST FOR
HISTORIC PRESERVATION
INTRODUCTION BY VIRGINIA AND LEE McALESTER
DESIGN BY JUSTINE STRASBERG

Produced by The Miller Press, Inc.

BANTAM BOOKS · TORONTO · NEW YORK · LONDON · SYDNEY · AUCKLAND

3 1901 02867 5181

THE FARMHOUSE

———————

A Bantam Book / October 1987

All rights reserved.
Copyright © 1987 by The Miller Press, Inc.
Jacket and interior photographs copyright © 1987 by Dennis Krukowski.
This book may not be reproduced in whole or in part, by
mimeograph or any other means, without permission.
For information address: Bantam Books, Inc.

Library of Congress Cataloging-in-Publication Data

Irvine, Chippy.
The farmhouse.

(American design)
Bibliography: p. 241
1. Farmhouses—United States. 2. Vernacular
architecture—United States. I. Krukowski, Dennis.
II. Title. III. Series.
NA8208.5.178   1987   728'.67'0973   86-47892
ISBN 0-553-05199-7

Published simultaneously in the United States and Canada
Bantam Books are published by Bantam Books, Inc. Its
trademark, consisting of the words "Bantam Books" and the
portrayal of a rooster, is registered in U.S. Patent and Trade-
mark Office and in other countries. Marca Registrada. Ban-
tam Books, Inc., 666 Fifth Avenue, New York, New York
10103.

Printed in Italy by New Interlitho S.p.A. - Milan

0 9 8 7 6 5 4 3 2 1

*To the memory of my parents, the
Reverend Allan Godfrey Grime and
Gladys Mary Grime.*
—Chippy Irvine
*To my mother Nancy, and to my mentors
Albert Hadley and Gene Moore.*
—Dennis Krukowski

ACKNOWLEDGMENTS

In the search for locations for this book, the intent was to find farmhouses that would maintain a geographic balance and present a variety of farm types. Traditional family farms where an assortment of animals are raised and varied crops are cultivated are becoming rare. Many of today's farmers must balance their love of agriculture with income from other professions, but every one of the farm owners we visited, while keeping a canny eye on the future, has a deep-rooted interest in America's history and the values of the past.

Many thanks to the following farm owners or guardians who generously shared the beauty of their land and the privacy of their houses: Mr. and Mrs. James Lloyd Butler, Mr. and Mrs. Richard Evelyn Byrd, Mr. and Mrs. Jack Cook, Mr. and Mrs. René di Rosa, Mr. and Mrs. Edward Clifford Durell III, Ms. Normajean Johnson Ek, Mr. Charles Glasner, Mr. and Mrs. John Hettinger III and their family, Mr. Yancey Hughes, Mr. John V.P. Lassoe, Jr., Mr. Sanford Levy, Dr. and Mrs. David Martin, Mrs. Peggy McKinnie-Weaver and her sons, Thomas Jackson Weaver III and Frank A. McKinnie Weaver, Ms. Loey Ringquist, Mr. E. Barry Ryan, Ms. Brenda Klein Speight, Mr. and Mrs. Harry Wetzel and their family, and Mr. Robert Zion. To all those whose farmhouses came under consideration but, alas, did not find a place in this volume, a special thank-you.

It would have been impossible to compile this book without the help of those who unstintingly supplied historical information and social contacts. Among the many are, in particular: Eleanor Albert, Vernon Ballard, Wayne Bell, Gracelyn Blackmer, Reginald C. R. Bradbury, Richard Charnoff, William Clark, Ann Collins, Rachel Cox, Leamond Dean, Peter Dunning, Richard DeCamp, Joanne Ditmer, Ann Ferebee, Tom Fleming, Louise Gerdts, Sally Guthrie, Sherri Hackworth, Sally Hambrecht, Wendy Insinger, Pamela Kephart, John Klein, Richard Lavin, Caroline R. Lassoe, Richard Keith Langham, Margaret Lucas, Victoria Lynch, Diane Haddex, Ruth MacDowell, Gae Mitchell, Nancy O'Boyle, Tula Ortega, Mary Pezzaro, Jacqueline Rea, Priscilla Rea, Pipka Ulvilden, Brenda Wade, and Floyd Woodbeck. For generous hospitality, I'd like to thank Arnold Dobrin and Michael Vecchio, and for endlessly organizing our flights, Joan Seigel.

I am indebted to the following authors for their scholarly information: James Marston Fitch, David P. Handlin, Virginia and Lee McAlester, Allen G. Noble, Harold L. Peterson, and Carole Rifkind.

To those who helped to form this book I would like to express my personal thanks: to Angela Miller, Bridget Fraser, Jennie McGregor, and all the staff of The Miller Press; Coleen O'Shea of Bantam Books for help and direction; Gareth Esersky for introducing us; Dennis Krukowski for his puissant photographs and Justine Strasberg for her graceful design; Nicholas Delbanco for literary advice and contacts; Tom Seligson for helping me to write; Marilyn Schlansky and Patricia Semo of the Patterson Library, New York; and most of all to my husband, Keith Irvine, and my daughters, Emma and Jassy, who allowed me to journey off in search of these American farmhouses.

CHIPPY IRVINE

CONTENTS

The NORTHEAST
8

The SOUTH
74

The CENTRAL STATES

132

The WEST COAST

176

FOREWORD

The story of American historic preservation begins with the threatened destruction of our most famous farmhouse, Mount Vernon. More than 130 years ago, a business group announced plans to convert the historic mansion and estate into a manufacturing facility. In the storm of protest that followed, led by Ann Pamela Cunningham of Charleston, South Carolina, a social movement was formed and a national landmark was saved.

Not all farmhouses have the stature of George Washington's house, of course. A more common view might be the idyllic vision of a rolling rural landscape, a valley dominated by wooden barns and silos nestled near a big white farmhouse. Growing numbers of Americans recognize, though, that the ideal vision is threatened by the practices of modern agriculture. The decline in farm population, the use of giant machines to till and irrigate the soil, and depressed crop prices and land values all pose dire threats to the farmstead and the way of life it represents.

The destruction of thousands of unique barns and farmhouses, as well as the historical landscape itself, continues today all across America.

In the preservation movement, we recognize that these historic buildings symbolize the character of their communities. They tie us to the past and help us make the choices about what kind of a community we want. They are, in short, an irreplaceable link with the culture we live in.

In the words of the National Historic Preservation Act of 1966, preserving "the historical and cultural foundations of the nation" will "give a sense of orientation to the American people." Our heritage has a purpose and a usefulness in contemporary society. Saving fine old buildings, whether in big cities, on small town main streets, or in rural settings, and putting them back to work in economically viable ways make our communities better places to live.

In the American farmhouse, we find the roots of our vernacular architecture, as well as many of the landmark buildings where great men or women lived and great events took place. Early preservationists concerned themselves with the old buildings associated with famous individuals and events, with battles and heroic deeds. In these historic sites they created museums designed to inspire reverential and patriotic feelings. They made historic places fragile symbols of America's growth and development.

Today's preservationist still finds importance in preserving single buildings and landmarks. But preservation has entered the larger context of neighborhoods and historic districts. The ordinary American farmhouse, preserved in its rural setting, has much to teach about an area's past and much to give to future generations. The task is not to enshrine these survivors from an earlier age, but to find contemporary and economically viable uses for them.

The farmhouses in this book, of course, enjoy the best possible fate of all for old buildings: they are lovingly maintained in their original use as homesteads. Their owners know what millions of Americans have rediscovered, that our old buildings, whether rural or urban, in small towns or far from the bustle of commerce, are the true centerpieces of our community life.

The American farmhouse brings to memory thoughts of a simpler time of firm values and rustic virtues. As the former owner of an eighteenth-century farmhouse in New Hampshire, I know we have a lot to learn from these structures, whether architecturally simple or complex. The Farmhouse can contribute much to our understanding of the central role these historic structures hold in our history and in our lives today.

J. JACKSON WALTER, PRESIDENT
NATIONAL TRUST FOR HISTORIC
PRESERVATION

T H E

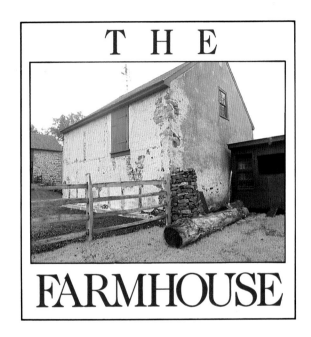

FARMHOUSE

INTRODUCTION

The first dwellings built by Europeans in America, as well as those constructed over the next two centuries by settlers on the continually moving edge of the frontier, were farmhouses. Subsistence agriculture is the essential occupation of wilderness pioneers, for they must self-produce everything needed for survival—food, clothing, and shelter.

Home and workplace are inseparable for the farm family and the dwelling itself is usually joined by outbuildings that provide shelter for crops, animals, equipment, workshops, and additional farm laborers. On smaller farms a single all-purpose barn often serves these functions but on larger holdings dozens of specialized outbuildings may be erected. The self-contained farm with its complex of accessory structures stands in sharp contrast to the usual urban house which serves only as a dwelling. In cities and towns the workplace—be it factory, office or shop—is normally at another location.

All houses, whether rural or urban, fall neatly into two great categories: some are built simply to provide basic shelter with little regard for changing fashion. These are called "folk" houses. Others are built in one of the many stylish architectural fashions that have been popular during America's long history. These are "styled" houses. Folk houses in any one area tend to be built in much the same way over a long period of time. The folk house builder typically depends on local building materials—stone, brick, or wood—and the construction techniques are passed down from father to son and from craftsman to apprentice.

Unlike these localized folk traditions, more distant influences are of great importance in planning a styled house. The latest house plan books, a new home seen on a recent trip, or the services of a specialized architect-designer may all come into play. A particular fashionable style typically spreads rather quickly throughout the entire country but persists for only a relatively short period of time. Like changing styles in clothing, architectural fashions are periodically replaced by more up-to-the-minute designs.

For the farmer, a concern for styled houses does not usually become possible until prosperity has passed the subsistence level and excess or "cash" crops are produced to be sold for monetary income.

With this money may come a concern for more fashionable living. The farmhouse then becomes not merely a comfortable shelter, but also a symbol of the farmer's prosperity and his taste for current design. A stylish new house may be built from scratch or, equally commonly, a simple folk house or older styled house is updated by a fashionable new addition or remodeling.

Among the fascinating features of The Farmhouse is its careful tracing of the evolution of each house discussed—from first construction to the current dwelling seen today in the delightful photographs. In addition to historical background on the families that have built and lived in each home, the text emphasizes how they have transformed their dwellings into their present form. By studying the evolution of these seventeen houses, house-watchers will learn much to help in deciphering the building history of other houses.

The Farmhouse *treats seventeen superb dwellings that include original folk houses, original styled houses, and earlier houses that have received later stylistic additions and remodelings. Five examples—The House on the Freer Patent, Bilyeu Farm, Yancy Hughes' Dog Trot House, Ek Trädet and Faraway Ranch—all began as, and remain, essentially folk houses, although some were built or reconstructed in several stages. The first two—The House on the Freer Patent (page 31) and Bilyeu Farm (page 52)—are quite different examples of early Dutch folk building traditions. The other three—Yancy Hughes' Dog Trot House (page 116), Ek Trädet (page 141) and the original portion of Faraway Ranch (page 153)—are examples of differing early log building techniques. Two others—Akindale Farm (page 41) and Greenwood Farm (page 16)—began as large wooden-framed folk houses and have had later additions of shingle siding, new porches, or door surrounds that have changed their appearance even though these "up-datings" made little attempt to recast the houses in a specific fashionable style. Country Homestead (page 164) and Alexander Valley Vineyards (page 183) are hybrid "Folk Victorian" houses—symmetrical folk forms with elaborate Victorian porches attached to give them an up-to-date appearance.*

Three of the houses, Heritage Farms, Dellet Park and Piedra Blanca Rancho, were built as styled houses and each retains much of its original design today. Heritage Farm (page 104) and Dellet Park (page 122) are quite similar at first glance. Both have the elegant full height entry porch, with a triangular pediment above, that was first introduced by the pattern books of the Italian Renaissance architect Andrea Palladio (1508–1580). These porches were much favored by Thomas Jefferson who popularized them in this country. Although built at about the same time in the early 1830s, Heritage Farms, on the edge of the western frontier, has an elliptical fanlight over the door that was common in the Early Classical Revival style that was already becoming passé. Dellet Park, built in thriving southern Alabama, was more up-to-date. It has the rectangular pattern of lights (small window panes) surrounding the front door, that were typical of the new Greek Revival style that was then replacing the closely related Early Classical Revival. Piedra Blanca Rancho (page 218) is a styled Victorian house that combines Italianate and Gothic details into the West Coast version of the Stick style, which was popular in the 1860s and 1870s.

In contrast, Burgess Lea (page 63), Normandy Farm (page 95), and Rancho Santa Clara del Norte (page 208) all began as folk houses. Each was remodeled (or had a major addition in the case of Burgess Lea), which transformed them into the handsome Georgian, Gothic Revival and Neoclassical houses that we see today. Rosemont (page 80), originally built as a fashionable Federal house, later received a complete remodeling that transformed the facade into the Greek Revival style. Finally, Winery Lake (page 94) is an adaptive reuse of a non-domestic commercial building that was originally part of a winery.

These exceptional and diverse farm dwellings provide a capsule summary of the challenges faced by rural families of differing means in many parts of the United States through three long centuries. The construction, interior and exterior design, and outbuildings of each farm are discussed and related to the social, climatic and economic forces that produced them. Among the fascinating additional topics treated are the introduction of the silo (which made possible the great dairy farms of the Midwest), the disappearance of many extraordinarily tasty varieties of apples from the marketplace, the construction and evolution of log houses, and the development of differing types of floor coverings. The temptation in a book with such handsome photographs is to study the illustrations and assume that the text is the usual filler. Resist—because in this case the words are an informative match for the book's great visual appeal.

VIRGINIA AND LEE McALESTER, AUTHORS OF *A FIELD GUIDE TO AMERICAN HOUSES*

THE NORTHEAST

Europern settlers arriving in the American Northeast in the sixteenth, seventeenth, and eighteenth centuries had two priorities: to construct suitable shelters for themselves and their families, and to provide a reliable supply of food. From the start, therefore, every house that was built had to become, almost immediately, a self-sufficient farmhouse.

Lured by glowing tales of the New World, especially Captain John Smith's A Description of New England (1616); The Generall Historie of Virginia, New-England, and the Summer Isles (1624); and The True Travels, Adventures, and Observations of Captaine John Smith (1630), the English settlers in particular, arriving in Massachusetts, were unprepared, according to James Marston Fitch in American Building, for the bitterly cold winters and hot, parched summers, the unfamiliar mosquitoes, gnats, and flies, and the hostile Indians of the Algonquin tribes. These northeastern Indians were nomadic hunters who lived in quickly erected dwellings made of bent saplings

covered in bark, but the settlers, wanting to build on a more permanent basis, rejected these Indian structures as unsuitable. After a brief period of living in shelters often dug into the side of a hill, the colonists started to erect houses based on familiar European forms, adapting them as best they could to the new and far more violent climate.

The early architecture and interiors of the northeastern farmhouses developed as a result of the practical considerations of the climate. The ground-hugging saltbox houses, the small stone or brick houses, and the clay-and-straw insulated shingled houses were built with small window openings and low ceilings so that they could be efficiently heated during the long, grueling winter months. The style of these houses owed its appeal to the virtues of austerity and simplicity as practiced by the Puritans, the Quakers, and the Huguenots, and was a form of design that was brought to an unparalleled height in the rural compounds of the Shakers.

Stone was plentiful and the clay was suitable for brick making, and both materials were used; but to the New Englanders the miles of virgin forests were amazing, especially since most of England's woodlands had been depleted by the time of Elizabeth I's reign (1558–1603). Wood became America's foremost building material and remains so today.

No matter what their cultural background—Dutch, French, or English—the early pioneers in the Northeast farmed in order to live, for this was before American farms could be considered commercial ventures. By the eighteenth century, Fitch says: "It [the farmhouse] was a processing center of a network of facilities: icehouse, springhouse, well house, milk house, smokehouse, washhouse, root cellar, and woodpile. Further out lay the orbit of vegetable garden, orchard, cow barn, pigpen, chicken run, corncrib, haystack and barns. Beyond this lay the farm itself."

Fitch goes on to point out that farming was not by modern standards a very efficient industry. The family worked from dawn to dusk. There was little time for the formal education of children, and indeed, the tradition of a three-month summer vacation, which is firmly rooted in the American school system, is based on the one-time necessity of having all hands in the fields during the harvesting months. By contrast, today our specialized farming system is so efficient, farmers sometimes have to be subsidized in order not to produce.

The homesteaders had to be inventive in the ways they adapted their dwellings to this new environment. There was a continual labor shortage in the Northeast, so any shortcut or machine that could be devised to cut the work load was worth pursuing. This necessity for ingenuity led to the myriad patented labor-saving inventions found today in every American household. Also, the traditional avoidance of the use of large numbers of servants in the Northeast, although due in part to

the ideals of democracy, was largely a result of the ingrained habit of the settlers, who had to do all the work themselves.

Many of the modern conveniences we take for granted today can be traced back through the last 300 years to the first American farmhouses. Windows, for instance, were nonexistent in the earliest earth and sod dugouts. Some of the earliest frame houses might have used oiled cloth or paper to let in light when the family could not obtain glass. During the seventeenth century, when glass could be made only in small pieces, tiny diamond- or square-shaped pieces of glass were held in place by strips of soft lead; hence the term leaded windows. Glass was expensive to buy, and both the British Crown and local governments imposed a tax on it. As the century progressed, larger oblong panes began to be held in sash windows by thick wooden muntins and putty, usually in a twelve-over-twelve formation. Gradually the panes could be made bigger and the muntins smaller until by mid-nineteenth century, panes could be made large enough to glaze sashes in only one or two units. Each change of technology brought a change of style that allowed more light into the house until, in the renovations of the 1950s, huge "picture" windows became fashionable, such as those in Akindale Farm (page 40) and Normandy Farm (page 92), while at Bilyeu Farm (page 52), a whole wall of glass sliding doors was installed into the eighteenth-century house during a 1963 renovation.

In a book based entirely on paintings, prints, and drawings from Colonial times to the late Victorian, American Interiors, Harold L. Peterson says: "Few modern families would tolerate the light level that was the norm before the twentieth century." All serious farm work had to be accomplished in the daylight hours. Candles, the only artificial form of indoor light in the seventeenth and eighteenth centuries, had to be made on the farm and were costly to produce. Apart from being a fire hazard, candles dripped wax and had to be constantly trimmed. However, they also inspired decorative—and now romantic—artifacts such as candlesticks, wall sconces, candelabra, and chandeliers.

A breakthrough in lighting systems came with the whale trade around 1830, when whale oil became available for lamps. A cloth wick, a glass chimney, and a shade provided the form on which most of our present-day lamps—though electrified and in an infinite variety—are based. Lamp shades appeared as a useful and decorative feature. The whale-hunting industry, based in the American Northeast, was profitable but short-lived. In 1859 a petroleum well, dug in Pennsylvania, signaled the end of whale oil as a fuel. From then on, kerosene kept the lamps alight. Gas lighting, used in urban streets and in the city houses of the rich, was seldom feasible in rural areas and, in any case, was superseded by the advent of electricity by the turn of the century.

In the Northeast the need for heat has been a major spur to invention. Early colonial houses were characteristically built around enormous central chimneys in the crude style of medieval European houses. Though inefficient and smoky, these chimneys did radiate the heat more or less throughout the house. The huge fireplaces, often big enough to walk into, were used not only to heat the house, but for all the cooking, which was, no doubt a strenuous chore. Greenwood Farm, Burgess Lea, and Bilyeu Farm all possess these early fireplaces. In order for their heat to be effective, however, the houses were built small, with low ceilings and tiny window openings. As the construction of chimneys became more sophisticated during the eighteenth century, stonemasons learned to place strategic flues. Several separate fireplaces could be placed throughout the house instead of one all-purpose fireplace; this allowed fireplaces to become smaller and less smoky, and the decorative mantelpiece became a feature of many rooms.

It took the canny Benjamin Franklin to market an American first—the revolutionary and efficient Franklin stove—which appeared in Philadelphia in 1744. Christopher Sower of Germantown had invented one earlier, but his was not a commercial success. Franklin's stove differed from its European ancestors by being made of cast iron, the most modern material of its time. Prefabricated and easily assembled from a small number of standardized parts, the stove could be used for heating and cooking, was self-contained, relatively cheap, and could be installed almost anywhere because it was detached from the chimney. This stove was the forerunner of all modern stoves and furnaces, according to Fitch. Most farmhouses in the Northeast, at some point in the nineteenth century, sealed off their cumbersome, old-fashioned fireplaces and installed Franklin stoves. With the advent of oil- or gas-fired central heating, present-day farm owners can enjoy the luxury of reopening these venerable fireplaces, to use them for heat or for decorative atmosphere.

Stoves used only for cooking were not brought into the kitchen until the nineteenth century, along with sinks and running water. Before that, water was hand carried from an outside pump; clothes were washed outside or in a washhouse using homemade soap; and bathing was considered unhealthy. Benjamin Franklin invented a shoe-shaped sitz bath and cautiously recommended its use, but the relationship of health to bodily cleanliness was not seriously considered until the nineteenth century. Very few farmhouses had indoor bathrooms until the second half of the nineteenth century. The outhouse was a feature on every farm until recently, and is still used on many as a backup if the plumbing system fails. But American plumbing made rapid technical advances in the twentieth century, and bathrooms became readily available to most farm families.

Another great American innovation that has brought health and convenience within everyone's reach in this country, and altered the decor of the kitchen, is refrigeration. Fitch notes: "Though ice had been used for millennia to chill wines and freeze sherbets, its use in food preservation seems to have been almost an American invention." The springhouse—a small building enclosing a spring or brook, used for cooling milk and other products—was used on many farms. A fine example exists at Burgess Lea, Pennsylvania (page 6). But the farmer's wife could only preserve her milk for any length of time by turning it into butter or cheese. Meat could only be preserved by salting or smoking it, and the smokehouse with its fireplace and outside sink for washing and butchering the hogs still exists at the Country Homestead in Texas (page 171).

Fruits and vegetables could be preserved in various ways. Some could be dried, such as nuts, raisins, or sweet herbs; others could be preserved in vinegar to make condiments or pickles; others could be preserved in spirits, such as brandied peaches. Fruits were cooked with sugar to make jams or preserves, but sugar made from West Indian sugarcane was too expensive for the average early American farmer's budget. In New England the indigenous maple tree provided the farmer's wife with sugar, but in other parts of America sugar was obtained from corn, sorghum or "sugar grass," or from white sugar beets. Until the mason jar appeared in 1858, preserving fruits and vegetables was a complicated affair involving sealing the jars with melted wax or paper brushed with the white of an egg. This labor-saving device, patented by John L. Mason, consisted of a glass jar with a screw-top lid of metal or glass, which made the farm wife's job much simpler.

The icehouse became fairly common on prosperous farms. It would be filled with ice cut from nearby lakes. By the mid-nineteenth century, iceboxes or early refrigerators were being manufactured. Today no kitchen in America is without one, and they are often used as gigantic cupboards for every kind of foodstuff. In addition, rural homes have immense freezers crammed with produce such as whole sides of beef or venison to feed the family when the roads of the Northeast are snow blocked and groceries are unobtainable.

The early farm provided much more than just food for the family. Sheep were kept for their wool, which had to be sheared, combed, carded, spun, dyed, woven, cut, and stitched—all by hand—before it was transformed into garments or coverlets. Spindles, far from being the decorative country accessory of today, were essential to the household, for spinning the yarn was the most time-consuming part of fabric making. Every scrap left over was saved to make quilts, bedding, or rugs. Shoes—there was no differentiation between left and right—were cut and stitched from animal skins that had to be home tanned. Nails and horseshoes had to be forged, furniture built, and even coffins made for the family dead.

In addition to making candles, fabric, and clothes, preserving food, cooking, and cleaning, the farmer's wife also had to nurse her babies, the next generation needed to swell the labor force. She cared for the sick—for which she grew or found her own herbal remedies—and tended to the elderly and laid them out when they died.

Finally, in her spare time, she might have decorated her dwelling. From paintings, diaries, and letters, we can get some idea of what an early farmhouse in the Northeast looked like. The housewife, traditionally responsible for feathering the nest, must have made many design choices based on economics, current styles, and her own ingenuity and artistry.

If the farm was prosperous, the floors in the larger rooms might have been painted. Black-and-white checkered patterns imitating marble were popular. (In the renovation at Burgess Lea, page 64, a mustard-and-brown color was used.) Or the housewife might have painted a floorcloth that was made of cotton canvas and stretched from wall to wall. In the summer straw carpets were sometimes used, but all these methods of covering the floor were available only to the affluent. The average farmer's wife would have sprinkled sand on the floorboards in a decorative pattern. Floorboards in the earlier houses were often twelve to fifteen inches wide because they were cut from the larger, virgin trees. Hooked and braided rugs were made but, according to available illustrations, were less common than painted floorcloths.

Walls, if decorated at all, were much more likely to have been stenciled than papered. This was a do-it-yourself operation, popular around the end of the eighteenth and beginning of the nineteenth centuries. Wallpapers—often of scenic patterns—were expensive because they were usually imported and were suitable only for grand houses.

Upholstery, if any, was a makeshift affair. Wool "sluts"—scraps from the spindle rooms—or feathers from the poultry provided the stuffings for homespun coverings.

Nothing went to waste. Harold L. Peterson notes that a wastepaper basket is never seen in any pictures of rooms until the end of the nineteenth century. Paper was too precious to throw away. But there are strategically placed cuspidors in many of the major rooms, items seldom conspicuously in use today.

Each of the farmhouses shown in this northeastern section was built before the end of the eighteenth century. The farmhouse owners of today have been influenced to a greater or lesser extent by some knowledge of their houses' histories. In some cases, like Greenwood Farm, the same family has been in residence for more than 170 years. Each generation has added some furnishing or decoration to the rooms appropriate to their day. As E. F. Benson put it in As We Are: "The room was the creation of its successive owners; a long established home was evident in it, and though it bore the impression of incongruous, and sometimes terrible tastes, a historical and collective individuality had ordained it."

Thus inspired by the past, each of these northeastern farmhouses makes a different but definitely twentieth-century statement about American design for the country life. Built in separate states and of varied materials, all have in common owners who care about the land and making things grow. Whether never restored or recently renovated, each house conjures up the aroma of wood fires, well-oiled leather, dried herbs, and freshly baked bread, and an aesthetic based on the pre-industrial American ideals of thrift and hand labor.

GREENWOOD FARM

A COLONIAL NEW ENGLAND FARMHOUSE
IN THE BERKSHIRES OF MASSACHUSETTS

The first settlements in New England developed as towns, villages, or hamlets around a village green. According to David P. Handlin in *The American Home*: "This pattern of settlement did not last more than a few generations. . . . by the beginning of the eighteenth century some towns even began to sell some of their land as a source of revenue." By 1730 isolated individual farmsteads were not unusual.

Greenwood is such a farm, and descriptions of it have to include some of the characters who influenced its development. Built in the 1730s by an Englishman, Captain John Fellows, this house, now covered in brown shingles, is the oldest house in Berkshire County still on its original site, yet it attracts scant attention, having never been fully restored to reveal its early clapboarding.

The colonists from England erected these timber frame houses using the abundant oak of New England not only for framing but also for floors and siding. Heavy vertical and horizontal timbers were joined by mortise-and-tenon joints reinforced by wooden pegs. Between the vertical posts, smaller uprights, called studs, were added. Horizontal wall boards or overlapping clapboards were attached to the posts and studs. Since most of the New England colonists came from south-

Between the dirt road and Greenwood farmhouse (LEFT) is a roughly mowed field lined with towering locust trees. Considered excellent lightning conductors, these trees, indigenous to the East Coast of America, were often planted close to houses for protection.

Today cars follow a grassy drive from the main dirt road to the back of the house. The front door (RIGHT) is almost never used as an entrance, although on hot summer days the doors are opened up to welcome a breeze.

The parlor (BELOW) shows a lingering sense of formality from the past, due to the traditional parlor ingredients—piano, desk, portraits, candlesticks, and the set of Victorian parlor furniture. The rugs were hooked by Mrs. Greenwood. Above the piano, portraits of Squire John and Lucretia Ward were painted by the well-known folk limner Ammi Phillips, who worked in this area of Massachusetts.

Because of its proportions, it is believed that the early nineteenth-century dining room table was made especially for this room (RIGHT). On the sideboard is a collection of family silver, some of it dating from Squire John's time. Above it is a theorem painting by Frances Coe Taft, in a style that was fashionable in the 1830s and 1840s. The sword over the fireplace belonged to her second husband, Dr. Terry, who served in the Civil War. The green sash, now blackened with age, indicates he was a medic.

eastern England (the only part of that country where the weatherboarding of houses was a common practice), they must have brought this technique with them. Hugh Morrison, in *Early American Architecture*, notes that clapboards were exported to England from Plymouth within the first year of the colonists' arrival, testifying to the plentiful supply of American wood.

Greenwood Farm's clapboards were painted red, a common color at the time, and they are twelve to fifteen inches wide. Because of later additions to the house, the original clapboards are visible now only through the cellar doors. The natural shingles that now cover the house were a rustically fashionable addition in the nineteenth century. Shingled houses were a valid early style in other parts of the country (see Bilyeu Farm, page 52).

Captain Fellows' farmhouse was built in a saltbox style, so named because of the resemblance to early chests used for

storing salt. Often these houses came about because a rear lean-to shed was added after the main structure, giving them a distinctive silhouette with an asymmetrical gable roof. The chimney was central and served to heat several rooms. Though Greenwood Farm has had a new wing added, and the functions of various rooms inside have been altered, all the main original rooms are intact.

The initial lands covered 1,000 acres on which Captain Fellows grew wheat and corn and raised cattle and sheep. He fought in the French and Indian Wars and died in 1757. His is the earliest headstone in the family graveyard, which is located about half a mile from the house. His son, for whom the Captain built a house nearby, led the local American forces in the Revolutionary War and became known as the General. Promotions were casual, rapid, and often self-proclaimed during the war for independence, because the fighting force was so small and leaders had to be found quickly.

Squire John Ward and his wife, Lucretia, came from Cornwall, Connecticut, some twenty miles away and bought the farm in 1810. He was a surveyor by profession and became a gentleman farmer. Judging from the furniture and pictures that survive in the house from this time, the Wards were well-to-do and the farm prospered.

At some point during the early part of the nineteenth century, Squire John added the "new" wing. This provided the larger kitchen now in use—the first kitchen was what is now called the living room, which has an enormous fireplace once used for cooking—a bedroom downstairs, a small additional dining room, and a sewing room, which has now been converted into a tiny bathroom.

John and Lucretia's daughter, Elizabeth Ward, married Joseph Murphy Greenwood, a Brooklyn lawyer. By the time their son, James William, was about to marry, the farmlands had been divided into small strips, each belonging to different

Not a modern kitchen (RIGHT), despite the stove, refrigerator, and new sink, this, as in most old farms, is the hub of the house. In addition to Mrs. Greenwood's collection of teapots on the mantel, there is a shelf with a collection of eighteenth- and nineteenth-century jugs and, over the stove, bits and pieces of blue delft.

The small breakfast or dining room (BELOW) is used as a game room and to accommodate a bar. A collection of milk glass hens and pottery platters and tureens fill the corner cupboard.

Ward heirs. James William Greenwood's bride was the daughter of Frances Coe Taft, a strong-minded woman who had married the dashing Captain Alvarez de la Mesa. He fell in love with her at a Newport ball, and their courtship was conducted entirely in French, the only language they had in common. Eventually she learned Spanish, but evidently he never did learn to speak much English. Mrs. de la Mesa realized that the farm and its lands would be dissipated, because the Ward heirs only used it as a summer retreat and entrusted the running of the farm to a working farmer who lived there year-round. She bought the farm, which now consisted of 200 acres, and gave it to her daughter and son-in-law as a wedding present, buying it back, so to speak, into the family.

Captain Alvarez fought in the Civil War and suffered wounds that caused his death some years later. His widow married a Dr. Terry who had also served in the Civil War and whose sword now hangs over the fireplace in Greenwood Farm's dining room.

Mrs. de la Mesa's daughter, Lola de la Mesa Greenwood, had a strong influence on the look of the farmhouse. She disposed of much of the accumulated Victorian furniture and reinstalled the simple, earlier pieces that had been tucked out of sight. She collected old pewter and eighteenth- and early nineteenth-century export china made for the English and American markets, which she bought at auctions at a time when there was little interest in such pieces. She had a modern streak too and was the first in the neighborhood to drive a Model T.

Much of the original land that was part of the farm has been sold, but the family still retains 132 acres, forty-five of

Now called the living room, this was the original kitchen in the house. The central fireplace, used for heating and cooking, had been sealed off in the middle of the nineteenth century when the fashion for Franklin stoves prevailed. It was reopened by Mrs. Greenwood in the early twentieth century. Kitchen implements and old pieces of farm equipment are displayed by the fireplace. Mrs. Greenwood collected the old pewter and started the collection of bells hanging from the central beam.

Early pewter was collected by Mrs. Greenwood before colonial artifacts were generally appreciated.

A collection (RIGHT) of blue-and-white china—English, Chinese export, and American—clusters in a corner cupboard of the dining room.

Homemade cotton hangings adorn the early nineteenth-century four-poster bed in this tiny guest room. Many members of the Ward family have been rocked in the nineteenth-century American wooden cradle.

which are cleared and worked by a local farmer. Many of the outer buildings are also gone. The farmer's cottage that used to stand behind the farmhouse was moved some distance away, but it gradually disintegrated and was dismantled, as was a long, low sheep barn. A large cattle barn tragically caught fire in 1975, and a barn that housed two decaying carriages and was overrun with chickens is now gone. Still remaining is a functional outhouse, as well as a red-painted carriage barn.

Deceptively small when viewed from the dirt road, the main farmhouse has nine rooms on the ground floor—kitchen, living room, two bedrooms, hall, large bathroom (which had been the borning room, or the room where children were born), small bathroom (which had been the sewing room), breakfast room, and walk-in storeroom or pantry.

On the second floor are two large master bedrooms and one smaller bedroom, as well as three children's rooms tucked

This guest room was part of the "new" wing that Squire John added early in the nineteenth century.

under the eaves. A collector's dream of an attic forms the top floor, filled with years of accumulation—hoop skirts, Civil War uniforms, top hats, trunks, and beaded dresses.

Apart from necessary concessions to the twentieth century, such as the refrigerator and the television set, most of the furnishings have been used by many generations of the family. As Mrs. Greenwood said many times, "We don't *buy* antiques, we *have* antiques."

This is evident. The paneled bedroom closets are stacked with hand-stitched linens; the kitchen and dining room cupboards are filled with china. There's comfort in seeing the well-worn family possessions arranged for convenience and use more than for decorative effect. Sloping floorboards, doors that are no longer square—these are part of Greenwood Farm's magic, a charm that time has helped to create and, indeed, improve.

THE HOUSE ON THE FREER PATENT

A HUGUENOT FARMHOUSE IN NEW YORK'S HUDSON RIVER VALLEY

A brief account of the political and religious events that shaped the history of this house will help explain its simplicity. The Freer family (sometimes spelled Frere) were Huguenots, French Protestants who followed the theologies of John Calvin (1509–1564), who was born in France and originally named Jean Chauvin or Caulvin. The great champion of Protestants, Henri of Navarre, became a Catholic when he became king of France in 1589, admitting that *"Paris vaut bien une messe"* ("Paris is well worth a mass"), in the hope he could conciliate religious differences, but his reign made way for more persecution of the Huguenots. During the reign of Louis XIV (1643–1715), many fled from northern France to the Netherlands.

Still seeking freedom of faith, a group of Huguenots came to the New World and between 1660 and 1675 settled in Wiltwyck, now called Kingston, New York. According to Kenneth E. Hasbrouck, who wrote *The Street of the Huguenots*: "By 1677 they had gathered in sufficient numbers to request a grant of land from the English governor and on May 26, they purchased the land from the Schwangunk Indians. The grant of a tract was given to twelve men in the name of James, Duke of York" (who ruled England as James II from 1685 to 1688). The confirmation of this patent—a document making a conveyance or grant

The reconstructed porch design (LEFT) was based on local structures, including remnants of the original porch on the nearby Terwilliger house, now a museum. The new porch is all mortised, tenoned, and pegged in the old style. Gourds and bittersweet from the garden decorate the table. A woodpile is stacked for winter.

Outside the barn (RIGHT) a wooden wheelbarrow holds pots of autumn flowers.

A 1790 wooden Quaker house (ABOVE) has been moved to the Freer property to be restored and used as an antiques shop.

The creek (RIGHT) that runs by the Freer house flows gently, but when it reaches the Terwilliger house, another later Huguenot dwelling, it forms a waterfall that ran a sawmill in the 1750s.

The house on the Freer patent (FAR RIGHT) is a typical early eighteenth-century Ulster County stone house built by Dutch Huguenots. European houses built at this time would have been far more sophisticated. The house used to face the old wagon track, but now it looks out on gardens, woods, and the stream.

A brick-lined fireplace with a wood-burning stove stands on the original fieldstone hearth of the kitchen. On the William and Mary pine hutch table are Dutch delft plates, coin silver cutlery, and mochaware mugs. The chairs are an assembled set of 1740 bannister backs from New York State. The cat, Innes, sleeps on a settle that came from a house in Orange County, New York. The settle is rare because of its small size and unusual "lollipop" arms. On the mantel is a mixture of New York redware, pewter, delft, and a burl-wood bowl.

of public lands—was signed by Edmund Andros, colonial governor of New York, and the original patentees were Louis, Isaac, and Abraham Du Bois, Abraham and Jean Hasbrouck, Pierre Deyo, Antoine Crispell, Hugo Freer, Louis Bevier, and Simon and Andries LeFevre. Although most of the names were French, by then they had been influenced by the Dutch and Flemish cultures. Their land centered around New Paltz, on the fertile banks of the Wallkill River in the Hudson River Valley. Although many early Dutch settlements were eventually superseded by the English, in this area Dutch influence remains strong, and many of the early buildings have been preserved by the Huguenot Historical Society of New Paltz in Ulster County.

The buildings have survived also because they were made of stone and were therefore resistant to fire. Allen G. Noble, in *Wood, Brick & Stone*, writes: "The abundant Devonian limestones of Ulster County yielded not only an attractive and easily workable building stone, but a source of lime mortar as well. Furthermore, a locally available, dark-colored sandstone called *bluestone* was also employed in building." Stone became the natural material for these shelters; when heated, the houses retained warmth in winter, yet they remained cool in summer. Moreover, one strong man could build a stone house piece by piece, but it took at least two to frame a house.

Early morning light streams through the old Dutch doors into the kitchen (LEFT). A stoneware crock with a rare lyre decoration sits by a small 1789 cupboard. Both are from New York State. This crock was on display at the Museum of American Folk Art in a 1986 exhibit on music-oriented folk art. The painting above the cupboard shows the nearby town of Alligerville.

Although overscaled and somewhat formal for a small farmhouse, this Hudson Valley kas, or linen cupboard (ABOVE), dates from the early eighteenth century but now holds the trappings of modern life: stereo, record collection, and answering machine. On top of the kas are blue-and-white delft, Chinese pottery, and one orange jug that is English New Hall china.

Often these dwellings started as a single room with a Dutch double door. As Virginia and Lee McAlester write in their *Field Guide to American Houses*: "The double Dutch door was probably developed to keep out livestock (with the bottom section closed) while allowing light and air through the open top. This style of door is found in about half the surviving houses. From the early 18th century, the treatment of the door surround commonly reflected the Georgian and subsequent Adam styles of the English colonies." Other rooms might be added, also with doors, which explains why many of these stone houses have several doors along the same side. Chimneys were built into the gable ends. The stonework often stopped short of the gable and was finished off with horizontal rows of clapboard or shingles. In effect they were not unlike the medieval Walloon farmhouses of northern France or Belgium.

The house on the Freer patent is such a dwelling. In addition to the 1677 patent, the Freer family in 1715 received a land patent for several thousand acres from the newly crowned George I of England. One of Hugo's sons moved south of New Paltz and built his house on the patent around 1726. His daughter, Sarah, married Evert Terwilliger, who was the first of his family to settle in the colonies. Evert built a house nearby in 1738. A third house of the same type is set back in the woods, and the three houses encompass an area that became known as the Southend Farms.

In 1807 Colonel Hasbrouck, a Revolutionary officer who was a descendant of one of the original patentees, acquired all three houses. He leased them to tenant farmers while he built himself a large Federal house, Locust Lawn, next to the Terwilliger house. He owned so many acres, it is said he could walk from his house to the Hudson River, eight miles, without leaving his land. Both the Hasbrouck and Terwilliger houses now belong to the Huguenot Historical Society and are open as museums. The society also owns the Street of the Huguenots in New Paltz, as well as the Little Wings bird sanctuary that is just opposite the Freer house.

Until 1974 the Freer house was used by tenant farmers whose main cash crops were corn and tomatoes. That year Sanford Levy, a graduate of the state university, began his search for a suitable house. The Freer house attracted him because the outside lines were so simple and obviously original.

Next to the window is a rare Oyster Bay Long Island blanket chest, set on four dogs, or unattached ball feet. Six layers of paint were removed with a piece of sharpened ebony before the original color of the chest was revealed. In the far corner a Hudson Valley kas, or cupboard, is in the process of being scraped down to the original paint. Displayed in the alcove above the fireplace is eighteenth-century Chinese export porcelain. The late eighteenth-century American wing chair is upholstered in a heavy cotton, jacquard woven cloth.

He and his partner, Charles Glasner, have spent several years restoring it faithfully, making it both authentic and comfortable.

The ground floor consists of two rooms, kitchen and parlor, laid over a cellar. It is thought, but not thoroughly authenticated, that these cellars, covered with brush, formed the first crude shelters for the early settlers. When the house was completed, slaves slept in the cellars, and to this day there are local New Paltz black families descended from the Huguenots' slaves; their family graves, along with those of local Indians, can be found in the Terwilliger cemetery.

A steep, enclosed staircase leads upstairs to what was originally an unpartitioned second floor that served as a grain storage area. Later the second floor was divided into bedrooms, but in the early days of the house, the family huddled downstairs in the parlor to sleep near the fire.

There are two chimneys set at either gable to accommodate the two fireplaces. No doubt the original fireplaces were primitive, just a stack of logs on a fieldstone hearth. Some of these early fireplaces can be seen in the Huguenot Historical Society buildings, where the chimneys started at the second floor, as in a medieval building. Although the present owner harbors the idea of restoring such a fireplace, he has desisted in view of the inconvenient smokiness that would result. By 1750 fireplaces had become smaller, the chimneys started lower down, being engineered to draw smoke out of the room.

Even in the early days, it is likely that the house had a porch. Mr. Levy discovered the remains of a Victorian gingerbread porch stacked up in the apple orchard. He also removed the iron railing and cement porch that was on the house when he bought it. The present porch, made of wood and constructed along simple lines, is historically accurate as well as practical.

Both porch and doors—typically one door for each room, of the original double Dutch style—face away from the present-day road. When the house was first built, the doors faced a wagon track that connected the Freer house with the Terwilliger house, but since then a paved road, Route 32, has been laid just behind the Freer house.

At some point in the house's history, the windows were changed from the original small panes to the two-over-two formation of the Civil War period. Mr. Levy restored the windows to the smaller panes of the original house, commissioning hand-joined frames and using only antique glass. It is almost impossible to tell the restored windows from the authentic old ones.

In the kitchen plasterboard that was nailed to the ceiling has been removed and the old beams once more exposed. The sink and cooking area have been adapted to meet twentieth-century needs. A local cabinetmaker built cherry cupboards, which also enclose the dishwasher and sink. Walls and ceiling are hung with antique baskets, bunches of herbs from the garden, wooden chopping boards, old molds, and unusual tin

Below an attic loft filled with eighteenth-century trunks and paper-covered hat boxes, rare because they are so fragile, is the landing bedroom (ABOVE). Two fan-back Windsor chairs still have their original green paint. At the end of the bed, an early Hudson River dower chest has interesting folk painting on the interior.

Antique toys (LEFT) are collected under the eaves of the attic bedroom. Most of the teddy bears date from the turn of the century, when they were popularized and named after President Theodore Roosevelt. The china-headed doll on the cupboard was made around 1860; the wax-faced doll on the bed is earlier, probably 1840. Covering the bed is an appliquéd album quilt. The earliest doll is a 1790 Queen Anne bedpost doll that was found locally; the most recent, a Fisher-Price fireman designed by a friend. At the back of the attic, a World War I flag welcomes home the "Men of Ulster County."

An 1830 Ulster County homespun jacquard coverlet (BELOW) was woven in Libertyville, a hamlet adjoining Jenkinstown, where the Freer house stands. The Federal period coverlet is unusual because of its central eagle motif. Topped by antique paper boxes, the 1790 cherry linen press came from New Paltz. This piece is rare because it is so small. Although it may appear big for the scale of this house, most presses were twice its size. The eighteenth-century looking glass next to it is unique because of its intricate carving, its small size, and because it once belonged to Governor George Clinton's family.

cookie cutters, while the cupboards are full of handsome antique platters that might have been used in such a farmhouse.

The other room that invariably gets the twentieth-century
treatment is the bathroom. Wedged into a tiny space upstairs
are a shower, toilet, and sink, while ingeniously fitted under
the eaves is a hot tub where the bather can look at aged wood
paneling as he relaxes.

Sandy Levy's regular job as a teacher in a nearby elemen-
tary school does not stunt his fascination for antiques, which
started when he was young and was encouraged by his parents.
When he was a teenager, his father, who likes to mend old
clocks, took him to an auction, and from then on, he was
hooked. He also developed an interest in folk music (in one of

the bedrooms is a hammer dulcimer, an instrument popular in
the early nineteeneth century, which he can play), and this led
to an appreciation of American folk art. It is not surprising that
Sandy Levy and Charles Glasner (an engineer by profession),
who team together in an antiques and decorating business,
have furnished the Freer house almost exclusively with artifacts from the Hudson Valley area.

Collectors' pieces abound. Several children's samplers not
only are from the region, but also have cross-stitched into
them a credit to the embroidery teacher: "Under the tutelage of
Eliza Ransom." One sampler shows a stylized but recognizable
neighborhood church that can still be seen from the Freer
house. In the early nineteenth century there was a fashion for

theorem paintings, usually bowls of fruit and flowers painted on fabric; on the Freer house landing is a rare one, unusual because the bowl is tilted at an odd angle. Near it is a Spencerian or calligraphic drawing of an eagle. In the hall are several nineteenth-century paintings by Hudson River artists that are exceptional because they are all of religious subjects. Downstairs are eighteenth- and nineteenth-century candlesticks and every sort of pottery a farmhouse might have used.

A bag of shards has been collected from digging in the garden. In it are pieces of clay pipes, New York redware, delft, 1840s English transfer, stoneware, blue Staffordshire, early American scraffito, and Canton china. There is even a pewter spoon with a heart back. These remains give a good indication of what the inhabitants of the Freer house dined with for the last 275 years. Mr. Levy has matched the shards with china that he has bought and used.

To expand the antiques business and keep it separate from their private lives, Mr. Levy and Mr. Glasner recently had a 1790s wooden house disassembled and moved five miles to their property, which they reassembled and restored clapboard by clapboard. A disarmingly simple structure, Quaker in origin, it looks just like the houses appliquéd on American quilts. This house, too, is being faithfully restored, and the antiques that will fill it should look quite at home.

Sage, marjoram, basil, dill, rosemary, various mints, parsley, and catnip are among the herbs that are picked all summer and dried for winter use (FAR LEFT).

A colorful trolley (LEFT) rests in a corner of the garden.

A pumpkin and weathered kitchen chair add color to an autumn setting (ABOVE).

AKINDALE FARM
HORSE BREEDING IN NEW YORK STATE

Until the end of World War II, the land that would become Akindale Farm was surrounded by dirt roads. Over 200 years ago, General George Washington rode along these same lanes. There is some evidence that Washington did indeed sleep at a neighboring farm, although we also know that he was quick to move when he found out his host was a Quaker pacifist and no help to his cause. Leaving the Quaker's farm, Washington made his temporary headquarters farther down the valley at the John Kane House, which is now a museum. This was the winter of 1778–1779, and conditions in the American army were as devastating as they had been a year earlier in Valley Forge, Pennsylvania. The soldiers were worn out and disorganized and food and supplies were scarce.

Washington chose this area as an army campsite because the hill where Akindale Farm now sits—the house was not built until after the Revolutionary War—commanded a high point between Boston and West Point. No one knew from which direction the British would attack, and the Americans waited on this high ridge in readiness. Most of the local civilians were Quakers, reported to be three thousand strong in the area. The army commandeered their meeting house as a hospital, and the Quakers quietly resorted to holding their meetings

A wraparound porch (LEFT) with fluted wooden columns was added to the house in 1926 by a dairy farmer named MacDowell.

Akindale Farm is named after Isaac Akin, a Quaker who built the original house (RIGHT) in 1789. The land covered 700 acres and was used for general farmsteading.

Amid the rolling fields nestles another farmhouse (ABOVE), which is home to the Akindale owners' son and his family. In an early Federal style, this house has a Palladian window centered in the clapboard exterior.

A flock of migrating birds pause at the lake (RIGHT) on their way south. Once rough wilderness and swampland, this lake and its island were landscaped in the 1970s by the present owner. In the distance can be seen one of the foaling barns.

in a nearby barn. A sharp rise behind the exact spot where Akindale Farm now sits became known as Purgatory Hill, named because of the hellish sufferings of the soldiers who had to haul cannons to the top by mules, all in the snow, ice, and mud of a New York State winter.

As it happened, there was no fighting in the vicinity, but the boredom of waiting was demoralizing. To raise the spirits of his troops, General Washington provided a feast of roast oxen for all his men, an event much recorded by local historians and known as the Great Barbecue.

In 1789 a Quaker named Isaac Akin built the first part of the present farm, at that time called Purgatory Farm. He probably built a barn first, which was the usual procedure. Often cows would be kept in one corner of the building while the family lived in another until the main house was completed. The farmhouse was a clapboard, two-story, colonial structure, with Georgian overtones in the placing of the chimneys and dormer windows and in the formality of the ground plan. It would have been considered a fine house and a credit to the owner.

The house was extended in 1844. Some of the original exterior clapboard can be seen inside the interior walls. Recently a discarded door saddle was discovered under a wooden tank in the attic. On it is handwritten: "This was put down in 1844 by John Corbin," and it names James Polk and Henry Clay, the

The chapel (TOP) was made of
local fieldstone. Inside, the
space has been turned into an
office (ABOVE). The fireplace was
designed by Mexican architect
Manuel Parra, and the picture of
the Akindale stallion above it is by
the well-known horse artist Tony
Alonzo.

43

Glass doors once divided this dining room (TOP) from the living room (LEFT). When the grand dining table is in full use, it is surrounded by fourteen Hitchcock chairs, each one slightly different. These were made at the Hitchcock factory in Riverton, Connecticut, during the first half of the nineteenth century. All the silver, crystal, china, and linen were bought in the 1950s. The horse painting by John Skeaping next to the sideboard was a gift.

The American Federal china cabinet (LEFT) is crowned with a carved eagle; unusually shaped astragals decorate the glass fronts, displaying early nineteenth-century English and American china. The elaborate mantel, designed in a confusion of styles, was installed in the 1950s in place of the earlier fieldstone hearth. Above it the painting of Newmarket is by New Zealand artist Peter Williams.

Once part of a long parlor boasting two fireplaces, this room (ABOVE) was divided in the 1950s into a guest bedroom at the back of the house and this snug study in the front. The pine paneling was hand stained. The rosette on the desk lamp was awarded to an Akindale yearling for "grace and beauty." Over the fireplace is an oil painting of the St. Francis chapel and some Akindale horses by Peter Williams. A duck decoy sits on the English mahogany butler's tray, which is mounted on a base.

presidential candidates for the two parties—the Democrats and the Coon-Whigs.

By the beginning of the twentieth century, the farm belonged to the Hoyt family. They donated the house and land to St. Bartholomew's Church in New York City, "In Memory of Alfred Hoyt," who had been a member of the vestry. The church used it as a fresh-air farm for city children and named it St. Francis Farm, although it was always referred to locally as "the fresh-air place." A chapel made of local fieldstone was erected near the farmhouse and dedicated in 1911 to St. Francis of Assisi—making it the only Episcopal church in the United States at that time to be dedicated to this saint.

The church sold the farm in 1926 to a Mr. G. Sherman MacDowell, who worked it as a dairy farm. He erected the silo and new barns, including a cow barn with stanchions for eighteen head of cattle.

In the house itself, the original narrow, steep staircase was altered to have a safer, more graceful descent. A formal dining room was created from a series of pantries and storage rooms, and a large window was installed to admit light. The craze for picture windows, which reached its zenith in the 1950s, was just beginning. At the same time the wraparound porch with fluted columns was added to the exterior.

By the late 1930s the locale was becoming fashionable, and the neighbors were no longer religious Quakers but socially prominent New York movers and shakers. Thomas

In the foreground on this upstairs landing (ABOVE) is a toy horse given to the present owner when he was a boy.

This rocking horse (RIGHT) from F.A.O. Schwarz was given to the present owner by his mother when he was a child. A new saddle and bridle are being made for it in Kentucky, to be ready for a grandchild's birthday.

46

A cheerful flower-sprigged pattern (LEFT) was chosen for the wallpaper and for the cotton-blend fabric on the chaise longue. The early nineteenth-century post beds are of American maple; the tall chest of drawers is American fruitwood. The Sheraton-style dressing table is English. The mantel was installed by a skilled local carpenter. Often called a Beau Brummell, the man's mahogany dressing stand is English (circa 1830) and supports a six-sided looking glass.

An office under the dormer windows (BELOW) has simple American maple furniture, handmade needlepoint cushions, flowers, and family photographs.

Dewey, Edward R. Murrow, and Lowell Thomas were among local property owners. The MacDowell farm was sold to Lowell Thomas, who, after only six months of ownership, sold it to Hugh Gibson, who was the American ambassador to Belgium and one of President Herbert Hoover's close friends. Although it was no longer operated as a working farm, a few animals were kept to retain a farmlike atmosphere.

The present owner's parents bought the farm from Ambassador Gibson in the mid-1940s. Their lives centered around New York City, and the farm became a summer and weekend retreat. The owner's mother supplied the house with its current abundance of furnishings, including china, silver, and linens. Keeping her favorite English antiques in New York City, she relegated the American maple furniture to the country. Likewise, when wall-to-wall carpeting became fashionable, her Oriental rugs were shipped to the farm. Expensive wallpapers and somber "Williamsburg" colors decorated the rooms.

Meanwhile, she encouraged her son's love of horses. If she came across an unusual toy horse, she bought it for him, and many of these can still be found in the house.

In 1973 New York State passed a tax law offering tremendous incentives for horse breeders because the state wanted to

encourage land use, as well as horse breeding. Through a natural progression of events, and thanks to the owner's finely cultivated love of horses, Akindale became a horse breeding farm.

At most times there are eighty horses on the farm, a number that surges during foaling time in the spring. The mares are kept outside all winter, for they are cold-weather animals and like the snow. For times when icy storms become too fierce, there are sheds with bedding. All the stables are immaculate, and the maintenance of the grounds is one of the most striking aspects of the farm. The trees are regularly pruned, the bushes clipped, and the fences mended.

The St. Francis chapel is now an office. The chapel had long since ceased to be an ecclesiastical building; the owner's mother had used it to store apples and his own children used to ride their tricycles around in it.

Because heating the chapel during the winter months would have been prohibitive without adequate insulation, this became the major expense in its renovation. The pseudo-Gothic windows and doors were retained, but most other evidence of a religious edifice has disappeared. At the eastern end, a bathroom and a kitchen have been installed on either side of a central round window. The large main room, which was the body of the chapel, is now used for conferences and entertaining. Tufted leather sofa and chairs, tables covered with horse-breeding publications, plants, pictures, and a large welcoming fireplace have transformed what was once a somber, stone-faced expanse into a comfortable reception area. For privacy, two small offices are situated on either side of the vestibule; one for the farm manager, the other for a secretary.

The owner's son and his family live in a handsome farmhouse on the Akindale property. Although a smaller house, it has an elegant facade centered around a Palladian window. Between the two houses, rolling green fields contoured with locust wood fences and a lake with an island have been masterfully landscaped. This land used to be swamp and wilderness and has since been tamed, yet the area retains the wild and natural elements that always prevailed. Migrating birds pause by the water, while deer share the fields with thoroughbred horses.

The interior of the main Akindale farmhouse strikes an easy balance between the formality necessary for serious horse-breeding transactions and the comfort of country family living. Equine and ornithological motifs abound. Many of the rooms were redecorated in the 1970s. They became lighter, brighter, and more informal than they had been in the 1950s. Most of the furnishings have been in the house for years, but upholstering the furniture with lighter ground chintzes and painting the walls white or sunny yellow have given every room a more cheerful, contemporary look. New mantelpieces have

The silo and cattle barns (RIGHT), *were built in 1926 when the property became a dairy farm.*

48

Akindale's horses graze in the
luxuriously landscaped pastures
that surround the farmhouse.

been installed in some rooms to replace those that were out of keeping with the age of the house, "not that all of them are historically accurate," the owner hastens to add.

A downstairs bathroom was added to the back of the entrance hall, which, together with a small bedroom next to it, makes a self-contained apartment for guests. Because the owners entertain frequently, they extended the kitchen, which is now large enough for breakfast and informal luncheons, and added to the housekeeper's wing.

Inherited furniture, much of it early nineteenth-century American pieces of a rather formal nature, has been integrated with the owner's favorite country-style furnishings. All of the

artwork has been collected over the years, with pride of place being given to paintings of the farm's most-loved horses. Many are by well-known artists in the racing world. Peter Williams, the New Zealand artist and sheep farmer, has visited Akindale Farm and painted alla prima landscapes with mares. A stallion might get a more Stubbs-like treatment from Tony Alonzo. This tradition of preserving the image of a favorite horse, which started in the eighteenth century with English country gentlemen, has been continued up to the present day.

Naive in comparison, and yet perhaps the most endearing equine image of all in the house, is the rocking horse on the landing—the horse that started it all.

The immaculately kept long barn (FAR LEFT) was built in 1926 to house cows when the property was used for dairy farming. It is now used as a horse barn.

Flush weatherboards with V-pointed ends are combined with clapboards to make a decorative end on the long barn (ABOVE).

Two of the barn kittens (LEFT) peer out from a bale of hay.

51

BILYEU FARM
A GENTLEMAN'S EIGHTEENTH-CENTURY SHINGLE FARMHOUSE IN NEW JERSEY

Seen from what is now the back of the house (LEFT), the gable shows an alarming tilt. This is not the fault of the camera but the way the house was originally constructed in order to accommodate the chimney. Adjoining the shingled house is the first half-timbered house, seen behind the porch, which is now modernized with sliding glass doors. The old cook house is just beyond that. The buttonwood tree (American sycamore) is more than 250 years old.

Mr. Zion's horse, Gallantry, looks out from the paddock in the old barn and stables (RIGHT).

The quarter-mile driveway from the road passes acres of young black pines laid out in neat, checkerboard patterns. Here in Monmouth County is the largest black pine nursery in New Jersey, and it belongs to landscape designer Robert L. Zion, author of *Trees for Architecture and Landscape* and designer of New York's Paley Park, the gardens of the Museum of Modern Art, and the planting around the Statue of Liberty restoration. The drive passes a horse barn and paddock, then climbs a hill where the farmhouse with its complex of buildings sits on the crest.

Looking for the perfect property, Mr. Zion wrote a two-page, single-spaced wish list. Among his many demands were an eighteenth-century house with dark shingles, set in the middle of land suitable for growing trees, a barn for horses, and a dirt road. He sent his list to Previews, a real estate agency that specialized, in the early 1960s, in European castles. He found it paid to go to the top. After two years the agency came up with exactly what he wanted, right down to the natural wood shingles.

A dirt trail, originally used by the Lenape Indians who inhabited the area, runs close by the farmhouse. Beyond the farmlands, the trail becomes the Burlington Path road.

The first half-timbered dwelling, built in the 1690s on a hundred-acre tract, was one-and-a-half stories high. The farm passed through the hands of several families. A large Dutch-style shingled house was built in 1720, just two feet away from the first building. This air space was left purposely to help insulate both houses. Two-and-a-half stories high, this house still has the original fish-scale, or curved-end, shingles, unusually long and generously overlapped to give a weather-resistant finish to the house. Curved shingles were harder to make but more efficient than square-cut ones because they never warped or turned up at the ends. Characteristically, the house had corner fireplaces, and the scars or blackened burn marks of these still show, long after they were replaced by nineteenth-century Franklin stoves.

Robert Zion acquired the farm from a Mr. Emley in 1963.

Emley had been a worker on the place when the owner, Lilly Bilyeu, who was dying, said she would give the whole farm to him if he paid off her debts. Emley did so, which is how he acquired the farm. Mr. Zion's purchase included 200 acres, horse barn, carriage house, icehouse, chicken coop, outhouse, and cook house. As a landscape architect, he saw possibilities others might have missed; he cut a gap in the boscage to create a vista, and made two ponds, using the displaced earth to build up a grass terrace outside the back of the house right next to a 250-year-old buttonwood tree. Mr. Zion says that Mr. Emley had feared that the tree, which was over one hundred feet high, might fall on his house, and so he had cut off the top. In spite of this lopping, the tree is still impressive and commands a greensward of rye grass in the fall and a planting of soybeans in the spring, put in especially to encourage grazing deer. This land-

scaping is in a typically English tradition, "of undulating grass that leads somewhere down to an irregularly shaped piece of water . . . of trees grouped casually, with cattle or deer about the slopes," as Hunt and Willis write in *The Genius of the Place*. No wonder that, when asked which landscape designers he most admires, Robert Zion nominates the eighteenth-century English innovators Lancelot ("Capability") Brown (1715–1783), who "transformed the stiff and geometric gardens of Tudor and Stuart England into an art that the rest of Europe imitated," and Humphrey Repton (1752–1818), whose contribution was to "reclaim gardens for social use and relate them again to the house they served."

Among the outer buildings, the carriage house has now become a garage, and the cook house, a high-tech home gym. The chicken coop houses Mr. Zion's Russian wolfhounds, and the barn, his horses. Also on the farm are a donkey, a pony, several affectionate stray dogs, and at least twelve barn cats.

It is easy to see that animals as well as trees are well loved here. Because Mr. Zion leads such a busy professional life, people seem to be a lower priority when he is at home. He considers solitude the greatest luxury. His saltwater pool—constructed more for sitting than for swimming—testifies to this. It is round and minute, intended for one person only. Describing how the pool came about, Mr. Zion says: "I had always lived near the sea, and the first day I came here I decided to drive to the ocean. Well, it took forever and I got two traffic tickets, so I turned around and came back and ordered the largest pool that could be brought to the site and made operative the same day."

He also computed how much salt would make the water feel just like the ocean, so now 1,400 pounds go into it every year—which sounds like more than was needed to destroy Carthage.

More recently, Zion and Breen Associates, Inc., his landscape and site-planning firm, have opened offices in nearby Imlaystown in a beautiful old mill house. Built in 1695 as an iron mill, it later became a grist and food mill and was owned at one point by Mordecai Lincoln, Abraham Lincoln's great-great grandfather. The builder, a Mr. Salter, died in 1720. Much of the mill burned down in 1898 but was rebuilt in the same style. Mr. Zion acknowledges that the move to the country has had an effect on the designs produced by his firm. In Manhattan there is a hard-edged look, he feels, but in the country a softer result. "And besides," he adds, "I can now ride a horse to work."

He has made considerable alterations to the farmhouse, joining the two separate structures into one and adding length to the smaller original building. The house ended about halfway into what is now the kitchen, where there was once a "cheese" or dairy room, which also accommodated the chimney of the Dutch oven. This space was extended and finished with a glass end and doors.

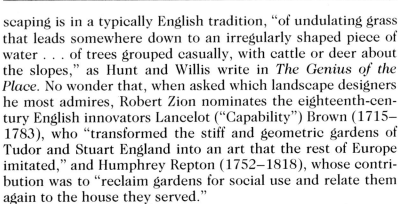

This cook house (FAR LEFT) *has now been converted into Mr. Zion's home gym. The restored icehouse* (LEFT) *was part of the farm complex. Vines cover part of the outhouse* (RIGHT).

To allow cross breezes but keep the animals out, Mr. Zion had Dutch doors (ABOVE) installed that were in keeping with the style of the house. Above the doors the window lights still have their original glass.

On either side of a table (RIGHT) holding modern blue-and-white spongeware are rare Windsor chairs that are actually from Windsor, England. The crude stone pestle and mortar were found together near the house and are used here as a doorstop.

The larger part of the house looks more as it would have in the past. Here Mr. Zion was careful to get the proportions of the windows right. When the house was originally built, panes of glass were smaller and muntins were bigger, although windows came to be glazed with panes of increasing size as glass-making techniques improved and costs decreased. To recapture the authentic look inexpensively, he added three-quarter-inch-wide tape around the frames, then painted it over. The effect is particularly accurate at night when the house is lit up.

Questioned about the unorthodox but successful color of the shutters and window frames, a neutral golden brown, Mr. Zion says he picks what pleases him. A house, he insists, should be an organic thing, changing with the times. He thinks it a mistake to be too much of a stickler for historical accuracy except in a museum.

Even on the outside of the house, he cannot resist his love of animals. A wren house nestles under each window. They are tiny, friendly birds, and the entrance hole is just big enough for

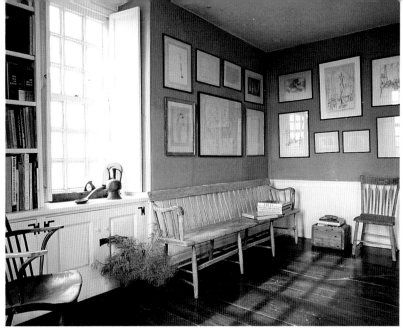

The original parlor (TOP) is now used as a library. The bench, bought especially for its paint color, was scraped down to the natural wood by a well-meaning friend by mistake. The collection of drawings includes work by Giacometti, Morandi, and Picasso. A tomahawk found in the garden sits on a box of books.

Over the mantel in a small upstairs bedroom (ABOVE LEFT) is a collection of painted decoys, a gilded angel from Spain, and an early nineteenth-century sampler. The desktop was found in the attic. It sits on a hand-carved piano stool that also belonged to the farm; the piano that it accompanied is now in the Brooklyn Museum.

A downstairs guest room (ABOVE RIGHT) has early nineteenth-century Hepplewhite-style post beds of American maple. The three owls on the mantel originally were bought to scare the pigeons from the horse barn.

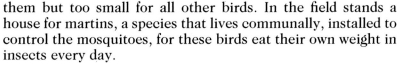

them but too small for all other birds. In the field stands a house for martins, a species that lives communally, installed to control the mosquitoes, for these birds eat their own weight in insects every day.

Once inside, there is no mistaking that this is the house of a designer. The simple, sparse hall leads into a truly mid-twentieth-century living room. The second floor of the original building has been removed, letting the chimney soar into the rafters like a piece of sculpture. When Mr. Zion bought the house, the fireplace had been blocked off. Breaking through, he found all the original fire tools, cauldrons, iron pots, bed warmer, undisturbed.

He joined the two buildings together by roofing over the gap and removing one wall, leaving the shingled wall intact on the interior. Here one can examine the detailing of the fish-scale shingles. As an interesting historical detail, Mr. Zion left part of the mud-and-straw mixture used for insulation in the wall completely uncovered behind a green shutter by the door-

Originally on the outside of the house, this early eighteenth-century shingled wall gives texture to the twentieth-century living room. The shutters flanking the doorway were found in the attic.

Slaves originally slept on the half-second floor of the older building. The floor has been removed to display the sculptural quality of the chimney and roof beams (RIGHT).

way. A scar on the wall shows where the second story used to be. This shingle-covered wall provides a wonderfully textured background for an eclectic mix of objects: a seventeenth-century Spanish carved-wood Virgin (her Child is on the piano), a grandfather clock, and a three-dimensional grasshopper weather vane, bought on Charles Street in Boston. Having been told this last piece of folk art was worth quite a bit, he took it to Sotheby's to be auctioned. However, as the sale came up, Mr. Zion felt its absence more and more and ended up bidding to get it back.

Bits and pieces of farm implements found lying around on the grass outside now form a frieze down one wall. The designer's touch is apparent in their arrangement. The opposite wall comprises a series of glass screen doors. Beyond the chimney is a kitchen with a dining table and an efficiently equipped work area lit by pool-room lamps. Throughout this part of the house, the floors are of brick manufactured in Ohio, the dark, ironstone color called candlelight. The same brick in a module twice the size is used for the patio outside.

In the rest of the house, the rooms are the same size and shape as they were in the 1720 building: simple guest rooms, a large studio bedroom and bathroom, a long, low attic, and a parlor used as a library. In this room Mr. Zion displays the things that please him, and these include drawings, prints, family photographs, pieces of old and new sculpture, wood collages—several by artist Bernard Langlais—and Indian artifacts found nearby.

"I've always loved the outdoors and growing things," Mr. Zion says. After getting two business degrees at Harvard, he decided he did not care for pure business and returned to Harvard to study landscape design, which turned out to be his perfect métier. Finding the Bilyeu farm extended his career from being a landscape designer to also being a plantation owner. The farm had previously grown corn, potatoes, and, in the later years, soybeans; it had also had a sizable amount of acreage set aside for growing white pines. Robert Zion, landscaping New York's Co-Op City, discovered that he needed pine trees that were tolerant of salty sand. The most suitable species were Japanese black pine, which he had to bring all the way from California. Seeing the need for these trees on the East Coast prompted him to start up a nursery for black pines. Magnolias, too, are grown in his nursery, and he is proud to indicate that some were sent recently to the Smithsonian Institution. But he is quick to point out that he rarely uses his own trees on his design jobs. "That wouldn't be prudent," he says.

Robert Zion is a good example of someone who wants to preserve the best about this earth yet leave his own mark on the world. Bilyeu Farm is the recipient of and heir to all his skills and indeed will be for time to come. He has willed his farm to be a shelter for stray or disabled animals and, because of his concern for the ecology of the land, has made arrangements for his farmlands to stay green forever.

60

Contemporary green pool-table lamps illuminate the kitchen work unit containing sink, stove, and dishwasher. Farm implements on the wall were unearthed from the yard near the house and barn.

61

BURGESS LEA
APPLE ORCHARDS AND QUAKER STONE
IN PENNSYLVANIA'S BUCKS COUNTY

A sign greets you at the gateway: BURGESS LEA, 1689. The drive is flanked with healthy and well-pruned apple trees. The grounds abound with the tasteful neatness that has characterized many a Pennsylvania Quaker home for centuries. The fences are tidy, the paths edged with youthful boxwood shrubs. The house stands compact and solid, nestling on the banks of the nearby Delaware River. At first glance, Burgess Lea seems far too neat to be old. Indeed, since 1978 it has had new and youthful owners. But the Durells are only the third family to live on the farm since it was established at the end of the seventeenth century.

A farmhouse whose history spans three centuries, Burgess Lea has had an interesting though not so varied past. The original house on the site was built by Andrew Burgess, a Quaker who married the daughter of a well-known Bucks County Quaker family, the Paxsons, and the building later was called the Isaiah Paxson House.

Quakers had been settling in America for more than fifty years. In England they had been punished for refusing to attend the established church and pay tithes, to take oaths, become soldiers, have their marriages celebrated by the clergy, or remove their hats to people in authority. For these actions many men, women and children were thrown in jail. When

Ducks swim on the reflecting pond (LEFT), which was landscaped by the Durells and is supplied with water from the spring— which has never gone dry—that flows through the springhouse. Across the pond can be seen the brazier's house, said to be the oldest building on the farm.

Red-painted picket fences and flower-flanked brick walks lead past the springhouse to the farmhouse (RIGHT). On the roof is a pig-shaped weathervane.

Wooden geese, bought through the Antique Maine Digest, stand on the painted porch floor (RIGHT). Neat brick walkways, clipped box trees, and red-painted fences with ball-and-chain weighted gates testify to Burgess Lea's trim appearance.

they reached the New World, the Puritans in Massachusetts feared them as bearers of heresy, so numbers of the Friends were jailed upon arrival, and some hanged for insisting on their right to worship as they pleased. Threats and anti-Quaker laws only increased the Friends' zeal. English Quakers, who had been frequently jailed but never executed, were alarmed at the treatment meted out to their brothers and sisters in the colonies and appealed to Charles II, who immediately sent a mandamus ordering all Quakers in prison to be released.

Gradually Quaker colonies were established in Rhode Island, Maine, New Hampshire, and on Nantucket. A string of meetings developed between Connecticut and New York State

(the builder of Akindale Farm was a Quaker). Quaker movements expanded to Long Island and along the southern seaboard; first New Jersey, then Pennsylvania became sites of mass Quaker settlements.

The Quakers benefited from their good relations with the American Indians. This was particularly noticeable in New Jersey and Pennsylvania where Quakers were in a majority and could shape their own policy. William Penn's Treaty of Shackamaxon, made on the shores of the Delaware in November 1682—"the only treaty," according to Voltaire, "never sworn to and never broken"—lasted for seventy years. Ironically, it was Penn's own children who made the first breach in the

thriving and fair land policy. William Penn's son, Thomas, never more than a nominal Quaker, was eager to extract financial gain from his Pennsylvania land holdings. In 1686 his father had agreed with local Indian chiefs of the Minisink tribe of the Delaware to buy land in Bucks County as far as a man could walk in a day and a half. Both he and the Indians understood this to mean about thirty miles. Thomas turned to artifice. The story is told in *The Quiet Rebels* by Margaret Hope Bacon: "In 1737 two athletes were especially trained to make the 'walk' at record clip. To aid them further, underbrush was cut away, horses provided to carry supplies and boats to ferry them across streams. As a result the 'walk' was stretched to cover

The checkered wooden floor (FAR LEFT) was painted by Diane Durell and given three layers of polyurethane for protection. The floors of many early houses were painted to imitate European marble floors when marble was unobtainable or too costly. The rare, three-dimensional, apple-shaped weather vane, which came from New York, was bought as an emblem because Burgess Lea is an apple farm.

The Pennsylvania dower chest (LEFT) from Lancaster County is uncommon because of its three drawers instead of the usual two. A collection of American antique baskets includes hard-to-find colored ones. Above them is a Lancaster County scene by the contemporary folk painter David Ellinger.

Local quinces catch the light of the afternoon sun (ABOVE).

sixty miles." This included all the desired territory. The Walking Purchase has been remembered by the Indians as a synonym of perfidy ever since.

Meantime, the Pennsylvania Quakers had prospered. Their carefulness about truth earned them the reputation of being honest tradesmen, but because they refused to take oaths, government service and administrative jobs were closed to them. They entered the developing wool and cloth trades, banking, whaling—whale oil was about to challenge the use of candles and influence the shape of lamps—and the business of brewing, for then, like everyone else, Quakers drank beer, ale, and whisky in moderation. Their diligence, thrift, and sobriety soon made them wealthy. Many, like the owners of the Isaiah Paxson House, became prosperous farmers.

In 1810 the farm fell into the hands of another local Quaker family, the Johnsons. For the next 150 years they had possession until Edward Clifford Durell III and his wife, Diane, bought it in 1978 from Mrs. Hartmann, who was a Johnson by birth. Mrs. Hartmann had been loath to sell this prize of a house for fear of it falling into the hands of property developers who would not maintain both the farmlands and the buildings as they had always been.

Dating from the eighteenth century to the early twentieth century, a collection of mochaware (FAR LEFT) made in Leeds, England, has a contemporary, almost neo-Deco look, in spite of its age.

In the kitchen (LEFT) floorboards are made of siding from a barn in nearby Lancaster County; the red sides were turned downward and the natural wood upper sides were sanded and polished. The tin lighting fixtures and iron pot holder were made by a local craftsman. The mantel holds a collection of antique Pennsylvania redware. The fireplace itself had been plastered over in the nineteenth century, as so often happened in old houses, but has been restored using local fieldstone. A bread oven has been lovingly reinstated, complete with its traditional "squirrel tail" chimney on the other side of the wall, which was copied from the nearby Thompson Neeley House, now a museum.

Red Delicious apples on the eighteenth-century Pennsylvania tea table (ABOVE) are from the Burgess Lea orchards. Paneled alcoves displaying Canton china may once have had doors. Their key blocks and cornices are typical of Pennsylvania Quaker style.

The antique Pennsylvania Dutch cupboard, still retaining its original blue-green paint, is topped with old baskets and stacked with contemporary plates and goblets made of Armetale (by Wilton), a metal that looks like polished pewter and blends equally with country pottery or fine Canton china. On the mantel a collection of reproduction redware by Pennsylvania craftsman Lester Breininger includes the Durells' inscribed birthday platters. A lovely old fireback protects the chimney and holds the heat.

From the day they gained possession of the farm, the Durells' aim has been that of preservation and restoration. Every aspect of it has been researched and respected to maintain a house that is strictly characteristic of the Bucks County Quaker region. Digging into the farm's past, they decided to rename it after its first owner—hence Burgess Lea. The earliest structure on the property was probably a one-room stone building with a corner fireplace, a house that is still standing on its original site in front of the large old barn. Traditionally called the brazier's house because for many years it was used by a brass maker, the house probably first served as a dwelling. Around 1700 the first section of the main house was constructed. This now forms the central section of the existing house and comprises part of the present kitchen with a vast fireplace, the dining room, and a small bedroom above. A boxed staircase still joins the two floors, and many of the original features, such as the wooden hanging pegs in the upstairs bedroom, remain.

The first documented part of the house is the 1785 two-story addition on the barn side of the first house. The scale of both the exterior and the interior architecture reflects how the family grew and prospered over the intervening years. Referred to now as the "big end of the house," this addition was built according to a Quaker plan, sometimes called a two-thirds Georgian architectural scheme, which is typical of many Pennsylvania stone houses. Essentially this means that the end ad-

A collection of antique paper-covered boxes, tinware, toys, and contemporary Beatrix Potter figures mix happily in the children's room (LEFT).

Children's toys cuddle on an antique Pennsylvania Dutch dower chest (BOTTOM). A child-size quilt and homespun wool coverlet cover the bed. The rug is decorated with tulips, a Lancaster County motif.

To one side of the bed (BELOW) hangs a silhouette of Chip Durell as a boy. On the other side hangs a portrait of Diane Durell, painted by English artist Tom La Fontaine, who is also well known for his sporting paintings. Above the chest hangs a Pennsylvania fraktur wedding certificate.

dition represents two-thirds of a symmetrical Georgian house of the period and comprises the main entrance and rooms to one side. The front door opens into the main hallway and stairs, with two rooms leading off to one side. The first house, which is now the dining room, leads directly into this new wing.

The impressive front door has its original bull's-eye windows, installed to let light into the hall, and is capped by a formal Georgian pediment that shows the influence of nearby Philadelphia, which itself had been strongly influenced by Christopher Wren's London. By the time the English Quakers had established Philadelphia—"The City of Brotherly Love," as it was dubbed—London, following the Great Fire of 1666, had

been rebuilt in a Georgian mode that well-to-do Quakers in the eighteenth century would have found familiar.

The steps up to the door are a Quaker feature, ascending three sides of the main step block. While gentlemen were permitted to stride boldly down the front of the steps, ladies modestly ascended and descended to the sides, discreetly shielding their ankles from the onlooking gaze of the gentlemen.

The Durells have preserved the Quaker preference for neatness, discretion, and quality in the renovation of their home. Wherever the eye falls, both inside and out, it meets with orderliness and ingenuity. This is particularly evident in the collection of outbuildings that scatter the grounds. Throughout Bucks, Lancaster, and Chester counties, old homes are characterized by their accompanying outbuildings; springhouses, smokehouses, and bake houses all were integral to farmsteads. Close to the main house at Burgess Lea is a Pennsylvania springhouse. Fed by gravity from a spring on higher ground, it provides running water and a cooling system and also supplies water to the duck pond in front of the barn.

Every year the orchards produce their crop of the standard apple species: Red and Golden Delicious, Cortland, McIntosh, and Winesap applies, plus the more unusual green July varieties, Transparent and Lodi, and fall Pippins. Peaches grown include White Hale, Red Haven, Raritan Rose, Blake Elberta, and Georgia Belle.

As the farm has been known locally for many generations for its apples and peaches, Diane Durell and some friends formed a cooperative group to work the orchards and sell the fruit. The large barn, showing by striations in its masonry and woodwork where enlargements have been added over the years, is used as a market. Although there are modern cooling systems in the barn now, the integrity of the original building has been faithfully maintained. Wood shingle barn hoods, typical of the county, have been restored, and the stonework repointed.

Other outbuildings include a carriage barn that is now used as a garage and two pool houses built by the Durells, complete with dovecotes on the roofs. They look as if they have been part of the surroundings for at least 200 years.

Linking this complex of outbuildings are newly built and well-maintained wooden fences. Those around the barnyard have gates designed with a graceful curved top, while the red-painted gates nearer the house operate on a practical, weighted, ball-and-chain system that the Durells observed on a visit to Williamsburg and had duplicated for their garden.

The same orderliness combined with practicality fills the house, in spite of the Durells' passion for collecting. Diane Durell came from the South and from a family who preferred new things around them. Meeting Chip Durell, who had always collected Pennsylvania antiques, opened up a new way of seeing things. She became enamored of local antiques and is now as avid a collector as her husband. Chip Durell's father collected old guns and clocks, and these collections are found throughout the house. There is a comforting rhythm of ticking everywhere, and on the hour, a chorus of chimes. Chip Durell has an extensive and unusual collection of mochaware, which is a

70

This large old barn has been restored and is used as a storehouse and market for Burgess Lea's apples and peaches.

Fields of corn surround the farm and border the neatly cut grass of the orchard (LEFT).

heavy, buff-colored earthenware that was produced at Leeds in England from the late eighteenth to the early twentieth centuries. While there are many varieties of mochaware, it is generally characterized by its decoration of cream stripes and additional green, blue, yellow, or tan and black ornamentation, which can look remarkably contemporary. An impressive array of mugs, bowls, and sifters nestles in a cupboard set into the old kitchen wall, and other pieces are dotted about the house.

Diane Durell collects old baskets. Harry Hartman, a well-established Pennsylvania decorator, has helped her in her quest for the unusual collection that now occupies many a corner of the house. Birthdays, anniversaries, and Christmas all become welcome excuses to add to their treasures. Fragile paper-covered boxes, German frakturs (commemorative pictorial certificates), Canton china, Pennsylvania redware, dower chests, quilts, decoys, weather vanes, and a gaggle of wooden geese that are now standing on the painted porch—all these and many more are sought, cherished, and enjoyed.

This fresh and adventurous approach underlies the whole atmosphere of the house, which has a spirit of youth and enthusiasm and, above all, convenience. For example, the kitchen, probably the most used room in any farmhouse, is a model of modern practicality and yet retains a thoroughly old-fashioned air. It is this knack of setting old against new in such a way that both are enhanced which gives their home its unique blend of age and vitality.

Chip Durell, as a building contractor, is in the perfect profession to come up with solutions for living comfortably in an old house, and he has been full of good ideas. Replacing the standard enamel covering of the refrigerator with a sheet of plywood, which was then painted to match the woodwork of the nearby cupboards, is one such innovation. Perhaps more apparent than anything else are the ingenious and unusual lighting fixtures that are featured in every room. Advised by Harry Hartman, they hit upon contemporary reproduction designs of antique tin lamps and wall sconces, which are lit by tiny electric candle-like bulbs, each of which burns only four watts. Because they are so economical to burn, these lamps are left on all the time, casting an inviting and old-fashioned glow over the house, which is otherwise dark within. Chip Durell insisted that no wiring or light switches show anywhere so that all the walls and paneling would be clean and uninterrupted, a rare feature in any twentieth-century home.

Comfort, convenience, collections. Great pride of possessions. The ghosts of a deep-rooted Quaker sense of order and diligent hard work. These are the ingredients. If, at first glance, Burgess Lea appears to be too bandbox fresh, one soon observes a real love and scholarly interest in the charms of Pennsylvania's past, mixed with an optimism about its present. One is left with the feeling that Burgess Lea is almost 300 years young.

72

Baby box trees lead to the newly built pool house (LEFT), which is topped with a dovecote.

A birdhouse (TOP) attracts a community of martins who help to control insects.

Inside the picket-fenced complex, a swing (ABOVE) has been set up for the Durell children.

THE SOUTH

The plantation houses of the South were based on an aesthetic entirely different from that of the austere and simple North.

The first settlers in the South established their roots at Jamestown, Virginia. Profit was the motive behind immigration to this part of the New World. The warmer climate of the South was discovered to be ideal for the cultivation of a new cash crop, tobacco. In 1615 the gardens, fields, and even the streets of Jamestown were planted with tobacco, which became not only the staple crop but the principal currency of the colony. The Virginia settlers, though not necessarily wealthy or highborn, came mostly from England, and they soon established a system of landed estates, or plantations, often with the high profits from their tobacco business.

To the south of the tobacco belt, from North Carolina to Florida, it was quickly discovered that cotton could be grown, once the land was cleared of virgin forests. Some of the Crown's early land grants were vast and largely unsurveyed. The glowing

tales of the New World, as published by Captain John Smith and other early explorers, were intended to lure more settlers, but there were never enough workers to clear the land, plant, and cultivate, and local Indians were not willing to be hired to destroy their own forests. The plantation owners hit upon a new scheme to import laborers—slavery. Importing workers from Africa was a move that had a far greater long-range impact on the South than the settlers could ever have imagined.

To underscore the master and slave system, the main plantation house became ostentatiously large. By contrast, slaves lived in humble quarters or in separate log houses (see page 113, Heritage Hall, or page 114, Yancy Hughes' Dog-trot House). The Northerners never made so much of a distinction, probably because their profits were not so great and they never owned vast numbers of slaves. The family slaves employed in the North usually stayed in the same dwelling as their masters, sleeping upstairs (as at Bilyeu Farm, page 59) or in the cellar (as at the house on the Freer patent, page 36).

Many of the earliest substantial buildings of Virginia were Georgian in type, and restored versions of these can be seen in Williamsburg. But the usual image of a southern plantation is that of a wooden structure, painted white, that looks like a Greek or Roman temple. With the flourishing economy of the South in the early 1800s, style, as opposed to bare necessity, became possible. The climate allowed for taller buildings, higher ceilings, larger windows. The slave economy provided the labor and also allowed the white owner to become a "gentleman," if he was not one already. An ancestor of the Byrd family of Virginia (Rosemont, page 83), William Byrd II (1674–1744), starts his secret diary for February 8, 1709: "I rose at 5 o'clock this morning and read a chapter in Hebrew and 200 verses in Homer's Odyssey. . . . I read law in the morning and Italian in the afternoon," and on May 9 of the same year, "I rose at 5 o'clock and read two chapters in Hebrew and two leaves in Plutarch's Morals." Many of the early owners looked to England for their culture and sent their sons to school there to get an education in the classics, studying Latin and Greek.

Cultivated Americans began to show an interest in the architectural styles of these earlier civilizations, but it was not until the latter part of the eighteenth century that the Classical Revival house made a general appearance. Allen G. Noble in Wood, Brick, & Stone says much of the responsibility rests with America's first great architect, Thomas Jefferson, who was educated at a time when science and the humanities were not yet separated into two specialties. His talent and force of personality were sufficient to impress Roman architectural forms on a whole generation of American houses. Jefferson, raised on the classics and familiar with the architectural designs of Andrea Palladio, deliberately shunned the English Georgian style, which was popular at the time of the American Revolution. The Federal style, which was formulated after 1789 and was a further American development of Georgian, merely exchanged, in his view, English motifs for an eagle. But the Roman motifs—the projecting pediment, supported by Doric or Tuscan columns—embodied the idea of Roman greatness, echoing the earlier republic and giving the world a message that the new American nation was strong and permanent.

Closely following Jeffersonian classical architecture came the Greek Revival style around 1825 to 1860. The majority of southern plantation houses were built in this style, which evolved for several social and political reasons. Many intellectual groups in Europe and America had, according to Noble, "the erroneous and naive belief that the Romans had originated classical forms. Subsequently European scholars discovered that Roman styles were essentially derivatives of earlier Greek ones. Furthermore, the empire of Napoleon had adopted Roman forms, and promulgated the 'Empire style.' Thus Roman architecture became equated with imperialism, autocracy, and despotism in England and English North America." Finally, the Greek war of independence against the Turks provoked a national, if romantic, sympathy for anything Greek.

By the time the temple-form houses of the Classical and Greek Revival styles had run their course, the American Civil War put an end to the building of large plantation houses. Building in the South virtually came to a standstill for the duration of the War Between the States, and when the hostilities were ended, new styles had usurped the classical forms: the Gothic Revival, which was inspired by an urge to rekindle the beliefs of medieval Christianity, followed by the polyglot architectural forms loosely described as Victorian.

The interiors of the southern plantation houses were grand in comparison to the early north-eastern farmhouses. Heating a house was less important than keeping it cool. Balconies and porches, large hallways that could become breeze-ways, louvered windows that reached the floors, all became features. Venetian blinds made their first appearance in North America. Thomas Jefferson made a drawing of a Venetian blind that is now owned by the Massachusetts Historical Society; the Library of Congress owns another drawing by Jefferson of window drapery for the study at Monticello, 1808. Though a crude drawing, the design shows elaborate swags and festoons trimmed with tassels.

Wallpapers, many of them imported from France, England, or China, were advertised in the local newspapers and began to take the place of stenciled walls. The walls in humbler houses were given a coat of whitewash. Painted canvas floor-cloths, sometimes called ingram rugs, were used on the floors (see Dellet Park, page 127), and often, during the summer months, the carpets would be replaced by Canton or Madras straw matting. (Thomas Jefferson was said to have used the matting as a "crumb catcher" in the White House dining room during his two terms of office.) From about 1800 until well into this century, floors were often covered with Venetian carpet—a striped, nonpile floor covering that was inexpensive and machine made. Floorcloths, which originally were wall-to-wall, began to show the wood floors more and more as the nineteenth century progressed. And, of course, wealthier house owners started to buy imported carpets from France, England, and the Orient.

Furniture was often made on the plantations, but as soon as the owners could afford to, they bought "ready-made" or ordered furniture of a spe-cific size for their grander rooms. Homemade furniture was no longer fashionable in the nineteenth century, whereas matching suites were highly desirable; carried to an extreme, a bedroom "set" at Heritage Hall consists of a double bed, an armoire, a washstand, and two dressing tables, all in an impressively heavy mid-Victorian style (page 109). Ironically, the original made-on-the-plantation furniture, though often simple and crude, is now much sought after by dealers and buyers. These pieces are few and far between in the plantation houses, for they were frequently discarded or given to the servants as the new furniture from New York, Philadelphia, or England arrived during the heyday of plantation living in the 1840s and 1850s.

The War Between the States and Reconstruction following it all but halted building in the South until the waning days of the Gothic influence, but the farmhouses of the South, both humble and grand, have a unique and romantic style that is very much a part of our heritage.

ROSEMONT
ROLLING ORCHARDS IN CLARKE COUNTY, VIRGINIA

Rosemont stands on a hilltop in Berryville, not far from Winchester, the apple-growing center of the Shenandoah Valley. Surrounded by orchards, the imposing house overlooks a steeply sloping informal garden planted with flowering shrubs and trees backed with towering pines. Berryville itself is completely hidden by the foliage, so one looks beyond it over the orchards to the Blue Ridge Mountains.

Rosemont's grandeur cannot be understood without mention of most of the great family names of early Virginia. The house was built around 1804 by George Norris, who married Evelyn Wormeley, the daughter of a wealthy Tidewater family man, James Bowles Wormeley. The couple had been given the property as a wedding gift. George Norris was a justice of Frederick County, which was the name then given to the area. When Clarke County broke off in 1836 from Frederick County, he was made the presiding justice of the first court held in Clarke County and later became the first sheriff.

Clarke County was named after George Rogers Clark (1752–1818) of the famed Lewis and Clark Expedition. The *e* added onto the end of Clarke County was a clerk's mistake that has never been corrected.

Like Frederick County, Berryville also was rechristened.

Built in 1804, this manor house (LEFT) has had various additions over the years. The Greek Revival portico, added between 1840 and 1860, overlooks a magnificent view of the Blue Ridge Mountains. Vivid azaleas sprawl down the lawn from the porch steps in the spring; fine old trees and rare shrubs are placed about the informal garden.

Apple trees blossom in Rosemont's orchard (RIGHT).

Pillared archways (LEFT) *add grandeur to the huge central hallway's upstairs landing and are echoed by three tall, arched windows. On the ground floor of this two-story hall, a late eighteenth-century engraving shows George and Martha Washington receiving guests at their home in Mount Vernon. The desk to the left is a Governor Winthrop, and above it is a photograph of a statue of the present owner's father, Senator Harry F. Byrd, situated on the capitol grounds in Richmond, Virginia. The lamp and two vases on the side table to the right are of matching Lowestoft china.*

A desk in the entrance hall (RIGHT) *belonged to William Byrd II and is believed to have been made at the Byrds' ancestral home of Westover on the James River. Although the drawer handles are intact, all the escutcheons are missing. A framed American flag above the desk was carried by the famous explorer Admiral Richard Evelyn Byrd over the North and South Poles. To one side hangs his collection of medals, and pictures of this handsome and heroic man array the desk. The large purple flag is the standard for the state of Virginia. It depicts a woman as Freedom, stomping on the head of a prone man representing Tyranny, or England. The motto reads* Sic Semper Tyrannus, *"Thus Always To Tyrants."*

In 1782 Thomas Taylor Byrd (1752–1821) came to the Shenandoah Valley at a time when it was considered close to the frontier. He had served in the British army in the American Revolution. Feelings ran against him in Tidewater, Virginia, where his ancestral home, Westover, had been built by his eminent grandfather, William Byrd II. Fortunately he had been given 1,000 acres of land in Frederick County by an uncle, and since the Scotch-Irish settlers of the Shenandoah Valley had been less involved with the harassments of the British and their royal governors, they more easily forgave his service in the enemy army.

Thomas Taylor Byrd married Mary Anne Armistead of Hesse in Gloucester County and came to live near the hamlet of Battletown. The name Battletown was attributed to young Dan Morgan, later General Daniel Morgan of Revolutionary War fame, a tall, rough-hewn frontiersman who lived in the area and was known for his volatile temper. His trips into town often ended in fist fights outside the local pub. History remembers him as one of the four or five most valuable military men on the American side during the War of Independence. Battletown was renamed Berryville just in time to become a real battleground, as it was the site of several skirmishes between Yankees and Confederates during the Civil War.

A portrait of Thomas Taylor Byrd, painted when he was a child in England in the 1750s, sits over the mantel in the draw-

ing room at Rosemont. He is holding a bow and arrow, which the artist may have used as an indication that he was an American. He looks much the part of an English aristocrat, and he was known to long for his civilized schooldays in England.

Soon after Thomas Taylor Byrd came to the Shenandoah Valley, heirs and younger sons of the Tidewater tobacco planters, ignorant of the therapeutic effects of rotation farming, began leaving their worn-out fields for the fresher pastures of Frederick County. Gentleman farmers (ownership of 1,000 acres was considered too little to label oneself a planter) built very large houses in the area. Wealthy families, including Byrd's, arrived and built manor houses using architectural designs based on English style books.

Rosemont was built as a straightforward Federal wood-frame house by George Norris, although it has now been stuccoed over the wood. Greek Revival houses were becoming popular, and these temple-form houses were beginning to proliferate more than the simpler Georgian ones. The Norrises succumbed to the fashion, and sometime between 1840 and 1860 they added an imposing temple-like portico to the eastern facade of Rosemont. A huge gable pediment, supported by fluted Doric columns, was appended to the original house, as well as a veranda seventy feet long and twenty feet wide.

The Norris family lived in Rosemont until the end of the nineteenth century. After a quick succession of owners, Mr. and Mrs. J. Low Harriman bought it in 1909. The Harrimans brought the plumbing up to date and added a big wing with eight bedrooms, making a total of thirty-five rooms in the house. The grounds around the house were planted with rare shrubs, and more formal gardens were designed by an Italian landscape gardener imported by Mrs. Harriman. A driveway winds between tall oaks, tulip poplars, and maples up a gentle hill. Pink and white dogwoods and azaleas blossom on either side of the drive in the spring. A large carriage house, now used for storage, once sheltered the horse-drawn vehicles that drove around to the porticoed east front, delivering passengers to the impressive steps of the porch. The driveway now stops short of this entrance because, in Harriman's day, he did not like motor cars ruining the idyllic view or exhaust fumes smelling up the fresh air. When Senator Harry F. Byrd bought Rosemont in 1929, the lawns in front of the old carriage road became a landing pad for presidential helicopters.

Every generation of the Byrd family has been involved in public service, from the first William to his present descendants, but two personalities stand out in the twentieth century. These are Admiral Richard Evelyn Byrd, the explorer, and his brother Senator Harry Flood Byrd. A third brother named Thomas Bolling Byrd made the trio into Tom, Dick, and Harry.

Admiral Byrd made himself one of the authentic heroes of the American people. In 1926 he flew over the North Pole for the first time, and in 1929, the South Pole. He was the only recipient of four Congressional Medals of Honor.

On the mantel in this sunny but sedate drawing room (LEFT) is an antique place setting of Kutani ware brought back by the Richard Byrds from Japan. The cover of the Queen Anne bench by the fire is an original design; the needlepoint was worked by Mrs. Byrd's sister-in-law, Gretchen Byrd. Between the windows is a marble-topped Louis XV chest of drawers. The chest has a bombe front, and the interior frame is made of heavy oak veneered with kingwood and rosewood, decorated with heavy doré. On the chest is a Chinese porcelain lamp, a pair of Meissen figurines, and small enamel boxes depicting National Trust houses. Colored engravings of Old London and the Thames River by Boydell (1756) are in their original frames and glass. The chair covered in blue damask is an original Martha Washington chair. Flanking the Chippendale-style sofa is a pair of Chinese lamps on burled olive end tables. On the coffee table is a rose medallion bowl. The carpet is Kerman.

In this walnut-paneled dining room (ABOVE), the table is made from virgin mahogany and belonged to the late Mrs. Harry Byrd's family, the Beverleys. At one time the table had ten leaves and could seat forty people. In the past hundred years, many generations of Beverleys have sat at it; in this century Senator and Mrs. Byrd entertained President Kennedy as a guest here in 1962, and President Johnson in 1965. Many cabinet members, senators, and other eminent Washington figures have dined here. The handworked Italian lace tablecloth depicts classical figures, flowers, and cherubs. The peach-and-gold china echoes the peach velvet drapes. Matching urns from the same set can be seen on the mantel reflected in the mirror. The table is surrounded with Chippendale chairs. The carpet is Persian. Under the gold-leaf mirror that came from the Beverley house in Leesburg is a Hepplewhite sideboard, circa 1790. On it is Mrs. Richard Byrd's grandmother's silver tea set.

While Admiral Byrd was winning acclaim at the far ends of the earth, his brother Harry made Virginia his domain. He left school at the age of fifteen and took over the bankrupt Winchester paper, the *Evening Star*, which his father owned. (To this day the Byrd family owns several small newspapers, including the *Star*.) Having made the *Star* solvent, he took on a series of successful ventures, while also getting into the apple-harvesting business.

By 1911 Harry Byrd had saved enough capital to buy land for an orchard of his own. He went into partnership with the Reverend William Smith, the Episcopal minister, and bought his first bearing orchard, the Rosemont orchard. Part of it was land that his ancestor, Thomas Taylor Byrd, had settled in 1782. The main house still belonged to the Harrimans.

In contrast to today's limited crops, there were more than twenty-six varieties of apples in Byrd's orchards. He grew Ben Davises, Albemarle Pippins, Grime's Goldens, Staymens, Lowries, Winesaps, Wealthies, and Smokehouse apples, to mention a few. Each variety had its special quality; beauty of appearance did not correspond to flavor. Richard Byrd, the current pomologist and owner of Rosemont, says he could grow much more delicious fruit if customers did not insist on buying big red or golden apples.

If Harry Byrd's formal education had been short, his political education was conducted by experts. His father, his uncle, and other family members ran the Democratic party in the commonwealth of Virginia. Harry Byrd was elected to public office before he even voted. In 1908, at age twenty-one, he was elected to the Winchester city council. In 1915 he was elected to the state senate. When he was thirty-eight, he became the youngest governor of Virginia since Thomas Jefferson.

In 1929 he acquired the house he wanted most of all and loved until he died—the Rosemont house—which was set in the middle of the orchards he already owned. The Great Depression affected the Shenandoah Valley as everywhere else, and the foreign market, which had taken forty to fifty percent of the Byrds' crop, collapsed. Byrd could not give away the small, flavorful apples he had been growing for export.

A Federal four-poster bed (ABOVE) is tucked into the corner of this downstairs guest bedroom. Net canopies like the one on this bed were particularly popular in America from 1780 until 1820. A padded storage chest tucks under the bed, or it can be used as a step up into this high bed.

A charming example (LEFT) of an unaffected, practical, mildly old-fashioned guest bathroom. The seven-foot-long ball-footed bathtub sits beneath a shower curtain that is hung from a metal hoop and, when not in use, slung around a huge hook.

After assessing the situation with his brother Tom, who was associated with him in the apple business, Byrd tailored his crop to suit the domestic market. Many old varieties of apple trees were uprooted and replaced with the first color sports of Red and Golden Delicious that proved to be very successful. He was one of the first to begin packaging apples in crates, then later in cardboard boxes, rather than barrels. In 1938, 50,000 new trees were planted in a single orchard on their land. By then, with a total of 200,000 trees on 5,000 acres of land, the Byrds were believed to be the largest individual apple growers in the world; all this while Harry Byrd was making nationwide waves as the much-beloved, conservative United States senator from Virginia.

These days, Richard and his brother, Beverley Byrd, collaborate in running the great apple orchards. Richard Byrd and his wife, Helen Bradshaw Byrd, a Massachusetts-born Yankee with an ancestral heritage that goes back to colonial days, maintain the historic hospitality of Rosemont even more elegantly than the senator did. They have combined their inherited antiques so that the house's furnishings are not all of one region or period. Byrd family memorabilia fill the rooms; in addition to the Byrd coat of arms, there are portraits, photographs, and sketches of the family, past and present.

Although the downstairs reception rooms—the large hallway, the sedate drawing room, the comfortable library, and the formal dining room—are wonderful for entertaining (and the porch outside is ballroom scale and often used for dances), much of Rosemont's charm lies in the rooms that are tucked away.

For all its large scale and would-be grandeur, Rosemont retains an easy, unintimidating, informal air. Each generation has added to the accumulation of historical details, and the sum total adds up to a bright, airy, welcoming house. Its owners, in spite of their fame and fortunes in other pursuits, have always been firmly rooted in a love of the land, a love that is shared by their neighbors in Clarke County. "The land is an integral part of our life here," says Richard Byrd. "It is not a status symbol."

A nursery (ABOVE) is held in readiness for a visit from the Byrds' granddaughter. A hamper on the floor is full of wooden bricks and flash cards with numbers and letters. It also contains a Confederate flag, a gentle reminder of the Byrd family history.

Decorated in fresh blue and white, this upstairs bedroom (RIGHT) leads into its own bathroom and the screened-in sleeping porch, which can be seen through the glass doors. The Federal canopy bed has fluted posts. By the bed is an Empire side chair made in Massachusetts between 1820 and 1840. Family photographs cluster on the bedside table and the dressing table. Across the chaise longue lies an antique lace negligee.

One of the fascinating features of a grand mansion are the behind-the-scenes back rooms that help to maintain the "gracious life." Here the butler's pantry (LEFT) is the perfect place for arranging flowers. The sink, with its practical, high, curved faucets, and the surrounding draining board are entirely covered with copper.

A household of the size of Rosemont requires its own sewing, ironing, and household linens room (RIGHT). This is a no-nonsense area with a bare light bulb and curtainless window through which the light can stream onto plants that have been put here for the winter. This room is lined with closets and drawers full of linen sheets, lace curtains, quilts, coverlets, fragile lace nightgowns and peignoirs, and the accumulation of household linens that a large and bustling home collects.

A *view* (LEFT) *of Rosemont's garden as seen from the steps leading to the pillared porch.*

Until the advent of the automobile, the carriage house (TOP) *was used for the family's or for guests' horse-drawn vehicles. Now cars are parked outside the carriage house, which is used for storage.*

Delicate apple blossoms from Rosemont's orchards (ABOVE) *will produce the Red Delicious apples. The first commercial orchards in the Shenandoah Valley were planted in 1900. It takes ten years of growth before a tree is commercially viable. Many of the new plantings have dwarfing rootstocks to make them easier for pruning and harvesting.*

91

NORMANDY FARM
THE THOROUGHBRED HORSES
OF KENTUCKY

Think of Lexington, Kentucky, and you conjure up visions of rolling bluegrass and spirited thoroughbreds. Normandy Farm has the fields and horses, as well as two unusual features that sometimes bring uninvited visitors. The first is the horses' cemetery, which centers around a life-size bronze statue of Fairplay, sire of the champion Man O' War. The second is Normandy's barn.

One story of how this barn came about centers on its builder, Joseph E. Widener, who fought in France during World War I. During a particularly fierce battle in Normandy, his group hid in a barn. As the clock in the tower chimed out the passing hours, he swore to his companions that if he survived the night, he would build just such a barn when he got back to the United States. The story is somewhat dubious, for Widener was involved with the French racing scene long before most other American horsemen, and he became a close friend of a French horse breeder named Mme. Couturier. She had an identical barn in Normandy, so it is quite likely that he simply copied hers.

Built in 1933, the barn was part of Mr. Widener's 1,300-acre Elmendorf Farm. He obtained part of his land from J. "Ben Ali" Haggin, a man of Turkish descent who had made a fortune

A *dirt road* (LEFT) *divides Normandy Farm from the next estate.*

In *addition to horses, Normandy Farm raises Black Angus cattle* (RIGHT).

mining copper in Montana. The rest of the land came from the estate of John T. Hughes, who was related by marriage to J. B. McCreary, the governor of Kentucky. A road called Hughes Lane still runs by the farm.

The portion from the Haggin estate includes the present farmhouse, which in Haggin's time was used as a manager's residence and, in Mr. Widener's day, as a spillover house for guests.

Built in 1804 by Colonel Abraham Bird, the house was sold in 1825 to Robert P. Kenney. Mentioned in *Ante Bellum Houses of the Bluegrass*, where it is called the Kenney house, it is a simple two-story brick house with four windows and a central door on the ground floor and five windows on the second floor. An ell protrudes to the back of the house. It is fairly typical of the early Lafayette County brick houses, most of which, like the Kenney house, had quite ample proportions compared to the brick houses that were built later.

Robert Kenney's son, Matthew, sold the farmstead to James Kerr in 1878. A small plot of Kenney graves lies not far from the farmhouse. Both Kenney and Kerr were prominent citizens and well-known stockmen. During Mr. Kerr's ownership, the house was drastically remodeled into the Gothic style, then considered more fashionable, giving the house its present-day facade. James Kerr sold all his property to Ben Ali Haggin in 1901.

During the 1920s, Mr. Widener put in most of the fences, lanes, and bridges. He was apt to give abrupt and costly orders. His farm manager, Mr. Terry, remembers going down a particularly muddy road with him when Mr. Widener, annoyed, snapped, "Build a bridge here!" And, of course, it was immediately done.

The Widener estate was divided into three separate parts in the early 1950s. His residence, Elmendorf mansion, was demolished to avoid taxes. Only the front row of columns can still be seen.

Horse trainer and breeder E. Barry Ryan has owned Normandy Farm since 1951. He named the farm after the distinctive barn on the property. Born in New York and raised in Montreal, Mr. Ryan started riding when he was seven. His father owned a stable of horses. "I was taken to the races, and by the time I was seventeen I'd bought my own racing horse for all of $1,000," Mr. Ryan says. At age twenty he was training three horses on the Toronto circuit.

When E. Barry Ryan bought Normandy Farm, he found

The simple lines of the original 1804 brick house built by Colonel Abraham Bird have been obscured by the Gothic Revival remodeling of the 1880s, which gave the house its present-day facade with three front gables, double-bracketed cornice, and single-story porch with Tuscan (unfluted) columns.

Books in French and English line the walls of the library (FAR LEFT) but leave spaces for the horse paintings. Each bibelot on the mantel tells a story; a rare drawing, called a transformation, by Dr. William Archibald Spooner—famous for his "spoonerisms"—depicts a cock fight called The Rival Heroes, which when held up to a strong light shows the heads of Napoleon and the Duke of Wellington. Other objects include a large uncut amethyst that was picked right from the surface of the ground in Zimbabwe; the hoof of a horse named How mounted in silver; a crested cigarette box from Queen Elizabeth II, together with a Christmas card signed Elizabeth R and a note thanking Mr. Ryan for boarding her horses; a billiken carved by Alaskan Indians; and a ceremonial hammer—a gift from Japanese clients—purported to bring health and wealth to its owner.

Over the mantel in the dining room (ABOVE) is a picture of the champion jumper, Quick Pitch, painted by Peter Biegel in 1968. To its right is a painting by Sir Alfred Munnings entitled Silks and Satins of the Turf. The Chippendale-style dining room table and chairs are from England.

The early Georgian grandfather clock (LEFT) from England still keeps good time and shows the phases of the moon. The cityscapes and landscapes are French, most of them painted by Mr. Ryan's grandfather-in-law, René de Braux.

97

Silky ticking covers comfortable chairs and an ottoman in a guest bedroom (RIGHT). The American Federal post beds are carved mahogany. Beside the fireplace is a drawing by equine cartoonist, Pierre Bellocq.

Photographs of family and friends crowd the side tables in the master bedroom (FAR RIGHT). On the walls, paintings and drawings of horses and dogs are by Mr. Ryan's friend Peter Biegel. The canopy bed was made in America in the late eighteenth century; the fox pillow was needlepointed by a friend.

that breeding thoroughbreds had become as important to him as training them. The luxurious stables on his farm are also used for boarding and have housed many illustrious horses, including some belonging to Queen Elizabeth II of England.

Mr. Ryan's farmhouse looks very different from the structure built by Colonel Bird. Apart from the 1880s remodeled Gothic Revival front gables and single-story porch, the ell at the back was filled out. This was accomplished during Mr. Widener's ownership in order to add utility and mud rooms. Mr. Ryan has made minor alterations to the interior. In the library, a very dark room, a window and French door were put on either side of the fireplace, making it one of the most inviting rooms in the house. A large picture window was added to the dining room, a typical renovation of the 1950s. He also installed a bathroom next to the master bedroom and another small washroom and shower over the kitchen. As in most twentieth-century renovations, plenty of bathrooms are a priority.

Typical of many old houses, the huge fireplace in the kitchen had been cemented over. "I knew it was there," says Mr. Ryan, "because of the big wooden beam running across the top where the chimney, I guessed, must start. I restored it and it works perfectly."

He consulted an architect for these alterations, which, while preserving the feel of the house, have added to its comfort. The decor has a French touch along with the many equine motifs, because of his French Canadian childhood and because his wife is French. For instance, he feels that most Americans do not hang as many pictures on the walls as the French. He speaks French fluently and spends much of his time in France.

Many of his horse paintings, though, are by the Englishman Peter Biegel. They became friends, and the artist has often stayed with Mr. Ryan in Kentucky. Framed on a table in the library is a charmingly casual watercolor sketch of a Jack Russell terrier called Stretchworth, with his puppy Hadrian. The current dog in residence, Duchess, is Hadrian's mother. Many more formal paintings of dogs and horses by Peter Biegel are hanging throughout the house.

Adjoining the farmhouse is an office that is fondly dubbed "the Quonset hut." In some ways this is the hub of the farm, for the farmhouse proper springs into social activity mainly when there are important local events, such as the yearling sales. Nearby, a building that was once stables has been converted into an apartment and a garage.

The unusual Normandy barn is worthy of all the attention it gets. Its circular tower is constructed of brick, and it has a clock that chimes on the hour. The L-shaped wings are wood. Fanciful ceramic animals—cats chasing mice, storks and doves—decorate its slate roof. The twelve stalls make it unusually big and luxurious for the foaling horses who use it.

Another comfortable barn is a large U-shaped one with arched windows and a slate roof. Other less substantial wooden barns are on the property; one, used for brood mares, is a modified tobacco barn.

The undisputed ringleader of this complex of buildings and the elegant thoroughbreds that live there is Mr. Ryan himself—trainer, breeder, and member of the Jockey Club. "I'm not in the least important," he says, yet in Kentucky and the rest of the racing world he is spoken of with respect and affection.

The farm is named after this barn (LEFT), which was built in 1933. Designed in the style of the great barns of Normandy, France, the tower, constructed of brick, has a witch's hat turret and a clock that chimes out the hours.

Hay is stored in the loft of the Normandy barn (TOP). Shown here is one of the ceramic animals that ornament the slate roof.

A bright red tractor (ABOVE) in the courtyard of Normandy Farm's U-shaped barn adds color to a rainy day.

A life-size bronze statue of Fairplay (TOP), sculpted in 1929 by Laura Gardin Fraser, overlooks the graves of Fairplay and Mahubah, the sire and dam of the famous racehorse Man O' War. Inscribed at the base of the statue is the legend "His sons and daughters won in excess of 2,700,000 dollars. His grandsires and granddaughters and their produce won millions of dollars additional." Surrounding them are other Widener horses' gravestones. E. Barry Ryan's horses buried here are Firm Policy, Quick Pitch, and Bonnie Beryl, each with an appropriate gravestone. In a corner is a gravestone where Stretchworth, a Jack Russell terrier and the mate of the current house dog, Duchess, is buried.

Dormers set into a slate roof (ABOVE) frame doors from which bales of hay are thrown to the ground below to feed the horses.

A horse and handler (RIGHT) are silhouetted in this modified tobacco barn, now used for brood mares.

102

HERITAGE FARMS

PLANTATION STYLE IN
HICKORY VALLEY, TENNESSEE

The opposite of a manicured small holding, Heritage Farms of Hickory Valley cover thousands of acres. The main house, Heritage Hall, is reached after traveling over a mile of gravel and red Tennessee mud. The romantic portico pillars of the hall loom up, half hidden behind towering cedars. According to hearsay, a ghost haunts the house. Dogs in a nearby run bark. A timeworn brick path leads to the front door with its graceful fanlight.

The genius of the place, Peggy McKinnie-Weaver, explains that she and her two sons, Thomas Jackson Weaver III (often known as Jock) and Frank McKinnie Weaver (nicknamed Tag), have only owned the Hall for three years, though, since the McKinnies lived for many years in an adjoining plantation, for them it has been like coming home. There has been little time to do anything in the house itself but move in, so everything is simple and sparse in spite of the large scale and the atmosphere of southern grandeur.

Several Tennessee families, some still prominent in the area, received official land grants when Andrew Jackson signed the treaty with the Chickasaw Indians in 1818, though it is suspected that white settlers had been around as early as 1812. Holdings then, as now, were often in the thousands of acres. Much of the land was used to grow cotton. The region was also

Built of local wood by McKinnie Irion in 1832, Heritage Hall's Classical Revival facade (LEFT) is partly hidden by tall cedar trees. The upper porch is supported by the house only, while the four Tuscan pillars hold the gable front.

The morning sun streaks across the lake beside Heritage Hall (RIGHT).

The ceiling lamp in this large hallway (LEFT) used to hang in the parlor. Instead, a chandelier was suspended in this hall, slung on a pulley that looped through the ring just above the front door so that it could be lowered in order to light the candles. The mid-nineteenth-century American settle to the right used to be kept on the porch and had been painted green, but Mrs. McKinnie-Weaver scraped it down to the original wood and brought it indoors. The hexagonal American candlestand, circa 1840, belonged to Mrs. McKinnie-Weaver's mother. The bird's nest in the urn came from just outside the front door, where it fell from one of the tall cedars.

Used as Mrs. McKinnie-Weaver's study, the library (RIGHT) displays personal treasures—like the Punch and Judy puppets found in England—as well as books. The oval portrait of a child in the parlor beyond is of Mrs. McKinnie-Weaver's mother; it is a photograph that has been painted over with oil paints, which was a fashion in 1903.

famous for its timber, and today Hardeman County is known as the hardwood capital of the United States; indeed, the valley is named after the hickory tree, which provides wood for that mainstay of pioneering, the ax handle.

Very little is known about McKinnie Irion, who started the plantation in 1820, but he must have become wealthy to have erected such a substantial house as Heritage Hall by 1832. He was believed to be of Scotch-Irish descent, and he is buried some five miles away from the house. In 1835 the hall was sold to J. J. Polk, who was a cousin to the future President of the United States, James Knox Polk. The Polk family farmed the plantation until J. J.'s great-grandson sold the homestead in 1983, at which time it was absorbed into the adjoining McKinnie Plantation lands, which were known as Heritage Farms and had been established in 1820.

The exact connection between McKinnie Irion and the McKinnie family who owned the adjoining plantation is not known, although there would seem to be a link because of the name. Members of the McKinnie family became related to several of the other early established white families of the Old Line

district of Hardeman County. This twenty-five-mile stretch of highway refers to the stagecoach line of the 1830s and the railroad line of the 1840s that links the towns of Boliver (the county seat of Hardeman), Hickory Valley, and Grand Junction (so named because it was the hub or junction of several rail lines).

Peggy McKinnie-Weaver's great-grandfather, William Franklin Hancock, married a Miss Jones after his first wife (Peggy's great-grandmother), Kate Mask Hancock, died. Mr. Hancock and his new bride lived in Hancock Hall, which is another large plantation house in the area. Miss Jones had come from a wealthy family who had founded a plantation called Cedar Grove. According to historical records, this plantation held 250 slaves in 1850. In 1901 Hobart C. Ames, principal owner of the Ames Shovel and Tool Company of Easton, Massachusetts, purchased the Jones House and, embarking on a program of lease and purchase, eventually controlled 25,000 acres near Grand Junction. Renamed the Ames Plantation, this estate now hosts the National Field Trials Championship for bird dogs, as well as a land research facility for the benefit of the

University of Tennessee. Both the Ames Plantation and Hancock Hall are open to the public on certain days of the year, while Heritage Farms hosts the National Bird Hunters Association Trials and is the home of the Heritage Field Trial Association.

Heritage Hall was built in the Jeffersonian Classical Revival style. The basic form of the house is simple and plain, but it has an elaborate columned porch appended to the front modeled after the Palladian porticos so admired by Jefferson. The gable has a projecting pediment that is supported by Tuscan columns. Two small, single-storied wings on either side of the main body of the house, added in the 1930s, gave the house a big kitchen, laundry room, and mud room on one side, and an office and large bedroom suite on the other.

Out of necessity, most of the wood needed to build the original house was milled right on the plantation, although it is known that itinerant carpenters who specialized in certain fancy details traveled from one house to the next. The scrolled carving on the staircase and the bull's-eyes on the door corners both inside and out and on the mantels were probably worked by these craftsmen. It is known that glass for the windows was made on the premises. Some of the simpler pieces of furniture were also made on the plantation, and several still survive.

All the downstairs reception rooms, including the main hall, parlor, library, and large dining room, have twelve-foot ceilings, and floors made of the original heart of pine. This wood, from the virgin pine trees, is impervious to termites, either because of its hardness or because they dislike the taste of it. All the doors in the original part of the house fasten with

Used sometimes to entertain judges and winners of the field trials, the farm office (FAR LEFT) has a welcoming wood-burning fireplace. The Union Jack on the wall was Mrs. McKinnie-Weaver's sole wage for her first season of summer stock in Canada when she pursued her acting career. The rifle above the flag was used in the Civil War by her McKinnie ancestors. Probably the oldest piece of furniture in the house is the Chippendale-style desk in the far corner. A simple child's chair by the coffee table was made on the McKinnie Plantation for a great-grandfather, David McKinnie. Framed on the wall above the desk is the governor's seal, which was awarded to Heritage Farms in 1985 for exceptional service to the community.

A mammoth bed in the Rose Room (LEFT), as this guest bedroom is called, has nine-foot columns. Mrs. McKinnie-Weaver explains that she knows it should have a canopy but that she cannot remember ever seeing one on it. An armoire and wig dresser in the bedroom are in this same massive early Victorian style.

In a guest room (RIGHT) is a substantial Victorian suite made of oak, consisting of bed, washstand, and dressing table. All the furniture came from the McKinnie Plantation. This room is part of the wing that was added to Heritage Hall in 1936 and includes a bathroom and the farm office.

A sunset glows on the red earth of Tennessee (ABOVE).

Recently rescued from demolition from a hotel chain site, a small interdenominational chapel (RIGHT) was dedicated by Dr. Harrell Townsend in 1985 and is a quiet place for family or friends to meditate and pray.

solid brass hardware of a type that was evidently standard in the area in 1832 but is heavier and differently articulated from present-day locks.

Because Mrs. McKinnie-Weaver and her son Tag as the general manager have been so involved with the running of the plantation, they have had no time for elaborate decorating. This forced simplification suits the house. The scroll-carved and paneled woodwork has been painted white, and the walls have been covered with a white-on-white documentary paper designed circa 1832, when Heritage Hall was built. Much of the furniture is of a massive mid-Victorian nature and must have been bought as the McKinnies prospered. By the time of the Civil War, the aesthetic attitude to house decoration was no longer based on the virtue of necessity, as it had been in the early northeastern farmhouses, nor were furnishings home-made. According to David P. Handlin in The American Home, "The desired effect was to show that each room had been designed not through a process of accretion but instead in a co-ordinated manner. Furniture had to match and be arranged in suites."

The state of Tennessee was the last to secede from the Union before the Civil War and the first to rejoin after the Confederacy's defeat. Mrs. McKinnie-Weaver's great-grandfather heeded the advice of General Robert E. Lee, who requested that the southern states get back to normal commerce as fast as possible, and David McKinnie was one of the first to sign loyalty to the Union after the conflict—albeit in order to be able to trade more readily. The family still possesses this signed document.

The Polks who had owned Heritage Hall also owned many slaves before Emancipation and these slave quarters are still standing. Set away from the Hall, these quarters consist of a large one-story log building that is now called the Hunt Club and is used for entertaining.

Mrs. McKinnie-Weaver and her two sons have definite ideas about how a farm should be run today. Hard labor alone is not enough. Far from being old-fashioned, conservative farmers, they feel that, to survive, they have to be innovative. They believe in sophisticated vigilance and a serious study of the commodities market. They are always looking for new

crops and possibilities. Right now, a vineyard is under consideration. Both Jock and Tag Weaver are bankers, following in the footsteps of their great-grandfather, great-uncle, and grandfather, who were bank executives as well as farmers. Jock Weaver has just become the president of the Hard Rock Cafes of London, New York, Stockholm, and Dallas, but he values his roots in west Tennessee. Although Tag Weaver, the second son, is manager of Heritage Farms, his career in banking is accelerating, and much of the farm business is handled by Peggy McKinnie-Weaver. Cotton, red and white oak, hickory wood, corn, and soybeans are the main cash crops grown currently, and many tenant farmers live and work on the land.

All three McKinnie-Weavers share a love of the land and give time and effort to community activities. The Heritage Field Trials are a national sporting event where bird dogs— English pointers and setters—hunt for quail. The dogs are judged on speed, style, courage, and good manners. "He must be bold, snappy and spirited, and pleasingly governable," wrote Hobart Ames, who was for forty-five years the president of the Field Trials Association. Much of the sporting and social life in

this part of Tennessee revolves around these trials, from the grueling three-hour Grand Nationals held at the Ames Plantation in Grand Junction to the half-hour trials at Heritage Farms in Hickory Valley, which are judged in retrieving as well as pointing quails.

Peggy McKinnie-Weaver also donates her considerable energies to the Association for the Preservation of Tennessee Antiquities. "We're not all rhinestone cowboys here, as Nashville would have you believe. Tennessee has a rich history that is anything but flashy. That old southern feeling for family and land is strong."

There is a happy if somewhat improvised look about Heritage Hall, as if the house had been taken by surprise by the McKinnies. When Peggy McKinnie-Weaver used to come over to the house as a child, she always felt that it had an unhappy atmosphere, but when she moved in, she had a little word with the ghost. "I said, 'the McKinnies have always been happy people.' We came to an understanding, and since then the ghost seems to be quite pleased with the way things are going, and the house has been perfectly content."

In the evening after the dog trials, the horses used by the judges and gallery feed in the stables (LEFT) while their owners enjoy champagne in Heritage Hall. Cages of quail are also kept in the barn. These are used in the trials and are placed in the grass for the dogs to retrieve. Bobwhite quail hold close to the ground and do not fly readily up into the air, which makes them the perfect quail for this type of trial. The quail are provided by the Heritage Field Trials Association and bred especially for this once-a-year event. No game is hunted haphazardly on the hundred acres that the McKinnie-Weavers set aside for these trails. The small barn on the right houses the farm dogs.

Originally slave quarters, this log house (ABOVE) was once chinked with clay, which has been replaced with longer-lasting cement. Now the building is called the Hunt Club and is used for social gatherings. Nearby is a small landing strip for guests' airplanes.

YANCY HUGHES' DOG-TROT HOUSE
A COLLECTION OF ALABAMAN SIMPLICITY

The "dog-trot" is a breezeway between two simple rooms, or pens; here (LEFT) a door to the living room leads off one side of the passage.

A door on the second story (RIGHT) leads to a loft that can be used as a storage place or bedroom.

Farmhouses in the South are not all substantial plantation houses in the style of Normandy Farm, Rosemont, Dellet Park, or Heritage Hall, nor are all of them built in the Georgian, Classical Revival, or Greek Revival style. The people who provided most of the hard labor lived in humble dwellings. Sometimes these were no more than temporarily erected shacks, but more often—and these are the houses that have survived till today—they were built solidly, if crudely, of logs.

Log houses had been built in the North by Swedish, Finnish, and German settlers. They had come to America from countries that still had abundant supplies of wood, and the house built of logs was part of their culture. Variants of the Continental log house spread across the Midwest until the image of the log cabin became the symbol of the American pioneer. To the South, and more particularly the upland South—nothern Georgia, Alabama, Mississippi, and southern Tennessee—there developed several variations of log houses.

According to Allen G. Noble, the simplest of these was a simple square log cabin, sixteen to seventeen feet on each side. This measurement is the size of an English rod which was a standard dimension for English houses and barns. Often these log houses were one-and-a-half stories high, giving the cabin a

Yancy Hughes's collection of small houses (ABOVE), originally used by owners of small farms or tenant farmers, were all dismantled on their original land, brought to this site, and reassembled.

This breezeway, or dog-trot, connects the two rooms of this log house. The logs are 130 years old, but the ceiling has been newly restored.

tall silhouette. The top floor might be used for storage or sleeping, and the single room below used for everything else. A chimney would be built onto one gable end, and a single door situated on the side of the house but away from the chimney.

A second type of log house evolved because of the need for larger houses. Logs were too heavy to make a full second story easily, since most log houses were constructed by one or, at most, two men. A solution was to add another room (or pen) so that the chimney was then placed in the center of the two-room house. This became known as the saddlebag house.

A third variant was the dog-trot house. A second pen was erected in line with the original house but separated by a space of about eight to twelve feet, forming a passageway between them. A gable roof would be extended to cover both houses and the open space, which became called the dog trot, dog run, possum run, or breezeway. The roof might also be extended forward to enclose a porch in the front and sometimes at the back as well. It was a house ideally suited to the South, because the open passageway offered a cool yet protected place to carry on household chores and to hold evening gatherings and recreation.

Of the many types of wood used, oak and pine were most often chosen. Both are straight grained, and although oak is more durable, pine is more easily worked. Green, or unseasoned, wood was preferred because it was easier to work with the ax or the adz. All the timbers were hewn rather than sawed, and as no cut lumber was used, the builder could be independent of a sawmill. Sometimes the logs were rough hewn, or smoothed off on the sides, often to make the walls on the inside smoother and give the house more status. The logs

could also be left round with all the bark attached. This was often the case in the temporary shelters of the North, but the round log construction was harder to chink and make weatherproof. The distinction between a log house and a log cabin is often drawn here—the cabin being made of round or unhewn logs and the log house being made of rough-hewn, square-hewn, or plank-hewn logs.

The crucial part of the construction occurred where the logs met and were locked in at the corners. Various names were given to the different types of corner points, the most common being the saddle, V-notch, and half dovetail. Other varieties, such as the diamond, full dovetail, and the double notch, required more skill to accomplish. Some types of notches were secured by wooden pegs, such as the square notch or the half notch.

When cut lumber became readily available, a great many of these log dwellings were covered with weatherboards to make them more weatherproof and look less humble. From the 1980s point of view, the result has often been a loss of the original charm of the log structure.

The logs that were first used for this type of house were, of course, virgin timber. The size of the houses was always determined by the height of the trees but was rarely more than twenty-four feet; beyond that length the tree tapered off too much to be used. However, the wood for the house cost nothing; the land had to be cleared of trees in order to be cultivated, and so the only expense was for tools. The rest was an investment in hard labor.

Yancy Hughes was born into a farming family. As a teenager he worked on the family farm in Alabama because his father wanted his children to know all about farming. By the 1930s, however, it had become obvious that farming was no longer as lucrative a business in the South as it had been in his father's day, so Mr. Hughes hedged his bets by becoming a pharmacist and also working for a bank that made loans to farms. In 1951, assessing the Whittaker homestead in Madison County, Alabama, for the bank, Mr. Hughes discovered on the property a disused log house. Although it was deep in the woods, covered with weeds, and very much in need of repair, it was a perfect example of a dog-trot house. When he asked the

owner what he intended to do with it, the reply was short: "Wish I could get it out of the way!" Yancy Hughes could not resist the opportunity.

It took four of Mr. Hughes's farmhands two days just to clear a path through the woods to the house. Then they dismantled the building, log by log, loaded the pieces on a truck and carried them forty miles to Mr. Hughes's property in Decatur. There it was reconstructed, rechinked, and given a new ceiling. The fireplace was rebuilt from the original rocks, and it draws perfectly, heating the room efficiently.

Looking into the history of the house, Yancy Hughes discovered that it had been built around the 1860s by a black man named George Garth on some land that was owned by a Dr. Whittaker and his family. Possibly Garth was a tenant farmer, for the house was in an isolated area.

As Mr. Hughes went about his business with the bank, he discovered more of these simple old houses, and when they were no longer wanted, he bought them and moved them to his own property. Frequently the older houses were being discarded in favor of more modern, convenient dwellings. Now

The fireplace in the living room (LEFT) was reconstructed using the original limestone rocks. One door leads onto the porch, the other to the dog-trot that runs between the two rooms.

The interior walls of this bedroom (ABOVE) show the rough-hewn logs and cement chinking. The pine ceiling is new.

Yancy Hughes has several, all built after 1870 in a humble, rustic style. Collected purely as a hobby and because he admires their simplicity, these buildings are not used as dwellings but as cabins where guests can put up for the night or where his growing children can have parties. The furnishings are sparse, as befits their setting, often leftovers from his own house. Often these primitive farmhouses were furnished with roughly hewn and homemade pieces, discards from the larger houses. Nowadays taste and style have come full circle, and people prefer the ingenuous homemade artifacts to the ostentatious "bought" furniture that usurped them. Many is the antique dealer who goes searching for the artless little treasures that once were used in these simple log tenant houses.

A rakish collection of furniture is assembled on the screened-in porch.

Vertical boards and horizontal solid-hewn logs chinked with cement are used on this simple farm structure (RIGHT).

DELLET PARK

A PALLADIAN HOUSE IN CLAIBOURNE, ALABAMA

Southern Alabama was wild country until the early nineteenth century. The area did not become safe for settlers until Andrew Jackson subdued the Creek Indians in 1814. In 1817 Alabama was organized as a United States territory, and from then on, settlers started receiving land grants from the President. The city of Claibourne, on the bluff of the Alabama River, and the town of Perdue Hill, four miles away, were two of the earliest organized settlements. Claibourne, a city of 4,000 inhabitants in the 1820s, was severely hit by cholera, an illness spread by the drinking of contaminated water. Claibourne was struck repeatedly by epidemics of this disease, a major hazard of the time, which killed much of its population over the first half of the nineteenth century. Many of those remaining moved to Mobile for safety and thus became the founding families of that town.

Long before the Civil War, Claibourne's importance had waned. Perdue Hill, being farther from the river, evolved as the more important town, and its houses were built in the Greek Revival style that became popular from around 1825 to 1860. Dellet Park is the only major house left from the early days of Claibourne.

James Dellet was a judge from Philadelphia. He married Harriet Willison from Columbia, South Carolina, and together

Dellet Park (LEFT) was built between the years 1823 and 1830. Here it can be seen garlanded for Christmas. The large tree in front of the house is the only one left of an avenue of sycamores planted by Judge Dellet, the original owner.

Solid cypress trees from the area were used for the fluted porch pillars (RIGHT), which were carved by Judge Dellet's slaves.

they bought a tract of land by the Alabama River to develop as a major plantation. Cotton was chosen as the main cash crop, but other types of farming such as grain, vegetables, hardwood, and also some livestock were necessary to maintain the plantation's self-sufficiency. The judge also set up a law practice in the city of Claibourne, which was on the opposite bank of the river from their tract.

To be near his practice, the Dellets chose the site for their main house at the edge of Claibourne on a 250-acre lot. They built a villa (in the Latin sense of it being a country seat) with outbuildings and elaborate grounds, the largest of its kind in the area at the time. The design of the house was taken from Palladio's second book of architecture, part of a scientific treatise on architecture written in 1570, which was translated into many European languages and influenced many later architects. The precise rules and formulas given in the book were widely adopted, especially in England, and were basic in the formation of the Georgian style. Judge Dellet took his design even more directly from the original drawings by Andrea Palladio, but instead of building it in stone as the Italian architect intended, the Judge built it in cypress wood and virgin pine—called heart of pine. Both types of wood were abundant in Alabama and had to be cut to clear the land for farming.

The builder of the house, Laurence Campbell, came from Greenwich, Connecticut. He intended to read law with Judge Dellet, for in those days an apprentice system was not unusual and there were few law schools. Whether or not he became a lawyer is not recorded, but it is known that Mr. Campbell had been a master shipbuilder and that the Judge persuaded him, perhaps in lieu of teaching fees, to build his elaborate house. It was an ambitious undertaking, requiring all the shipbuilder's ingenuity and using nothing but local materials and the unskilled labor of the Judge's slaves. All the mill work involved in the building was done on the plantation, and the workers developed their own knives for the lathes. Probably all the glass used for the windows was also made on the estate, and Dellet Park still retains most of the original glass, which can be detected because the panes are pleasingly distorted.

The building was begun in 1823 but was not completed until 1830. While it was being built, the Judge and his wife lived temporarily in a log house nearby. Knowing the exact plans and measurements for all the rooms in the house, they were able to order furniture to their own specifications from the more sophisticated centers of cabinetmaking, such as New York and Philadelphia.

The Judge was already making his mark as a respectable and prosperous citizen. When, between 1824 and 1825, the Marquis de Lafayette came on his last visit to America, he stayed en route to New Orleans at Judge Dellet's plantation. A sumptuous meal—all French dishes, of course—was served on the dining room table that had been ordered from New York, and Lafayette sat on one of the Empire dining room chairs that

In the center of this round pond (LEFT) is a fountain that sends a jet of water forty feet into the air. Always trying out new places to have a fête champêtre, the present owners can lunch here, or in a grotto complete with a cupid, or among the 120 varieties of camellias that were planted in the 1920s and are now twenty feet tall.

These board-and-batten one-room buildings (ABOVE) once would house a whole family of slaves, without benefit of kitchen or bathroom. During this last century, tar paper made to look like bricks was used to protect them and assumed to be an improvement, but the wood underneath has rotted in many places.

This morning room is used for small luncheons. The secretary between the windows, ordered for the house by Judge Dellet and his wife, was made in Philadelphia and sent down by boat in the 1820s before Dellet Park was completed. The apricot Chinese silk curtains, donated by friends in Mobile, fitted the tall windows exactly. The black-and-gold Regency chairs came from New Orleans. The cane-seated American Empire armchairs are original to the house. The armchairs in klismos shape at the skirted table are from the dining room and were used at a banquet at Dellet Park honoring the Marquis de Lafayette in the 1820s.

are still in use at Dellet Park. He was by then an old man, but he gave a speech at the Claibourne town hall and afterward slept on the four-poster bed that is currently in one of Dellet Park's guest bedrooms—although the house was not finished at the time of the Marquis's visit and the bed was squeezed into the Judge's log house.

Judge Dellet became the first speaker of the house in Alabama, and thereafter he was elected senator and had to spend much of his time in Washington, D.C. When his wife died in 1830—of cancer, it is thought—he received many letters of condolence from high-ranking persons. These letters are still in the house at Dellet Park. The Judge also lost two of his children in a cholera epidemic.

Judge Dellet spent only a few years living in his house. After the death of his first wife, he married a woman who had been the governess of his sole surviving daughter, Emma. Emma did not approve of the union, and so, in compensation, he let her have Dellet Park for herself and her husband, Lymon Gibbons. The Judge built himself a new house across the river nearer his plantation, where he and the governess lived until he died in 1837. The family is buried in the camellia garden at Dellet Park.

Emma and Lymon Gibbons, a lawyer, went to Paris, where they lived during the reign of Napoleon III and the Empress Eugénie. Some of Emma's Parisian dresses are on display at the City Museum at Mobile. A receipt for just one of them—a taffeta day dress—shows that it cost a 1,000 dollars, an astounding amount for those days. Parisian fashion played a crucial role in a lady's status; it is said that Empress Eugénie once remarked "Worth and I rule Paris."

When Emma and her husband returned to America in the 1860s, they built a house in the more sophisticated town of Mobile. From that time onward, Dellet Park was used only as a summer residence and as a refuge from the yellow fever epidemics that plagued Mobile during the summer months. Fevers and cholera were to be a threat in the South throughout the century.

Slave conditions in the South were harsh. Whole families lived in single-room houses built away from the main house. Two of these buildings exist at Dellet Park to this day; they are built of batten and board, with wood porches and tin roofs. These slave quarters had neither kitchen nor bathroom nor any concession to privacy.

By contrast, the interiors of the big house were not only

grand but abounding with wonderful inventiveness. Every bedroom was planned from the start to have built-in closets. Extra closets for articles of clothing had pegs at the back for hanging coats or dresses and shelves inside for folded garments. These rather crude armoires were made on the plantation, and two of them have been relegated to the original kitchen building. Each bedroom had a simple couch or daybed where the gentlefolk could take a nap without disturbing the feather bed, which would have been made up early in the morning. These daybeds—there is one on the upstairs landing—had crude wooden frames and were covered with chintz stuffed with cotton from the fields. They were a homemade alternative to the strictly upholstered chaise longue.

Even more innovative was the bathroom that was included in the original plan of the house's interior. Situated at the back of the house on the ground floor, the "cabinet," as it was called, was conveniently placed for the servants to bring hot water from the outside kitchen to fill the tub. The zinc bath came from Paris and looks exactly like the bath in David's painting, *The Death of Marat.* The bathtub is now stored up in the attic. After a bath, the water was emptied through a plug and a hole

in the floor into hog-skin bags in the crawl space under the floorboards. These would be removed by the servants, thus allowing the bather complete privacy.

Dellet Park even had wall-to-wall carpeting. Considered high fashion at the time, this carpeting took the form of hand-painted canvas rugs bearing Classical Revival (rather than Victorian) designs. One is decorated with large acanthus leaves and roses in the center. Another, designed for the hall, has a blue-and-white design similar to patterns seen on Wedgwood china. These canvas floorcloths stayed in place right up until the 1920s, when, not surprisingly, they were found to be somewhat worn and were rolled up and stored away in the attic. Unfortunately, heavy furniture carelessly stacked on top has cracked them. But interior design goes in cycles, and once again canvas rugs are being painted today by skilled crafts people, inspired by many of these old patterns.

The only imported fixtures in the house were two mantels: a black marble one from Belgium in the library and a white Carrara marble one in the morning room. Both are of Classical Revival design.

Books belonging to the educated and well-read Dellet fam-

Shelves on the upstairs landing hold Judge Dellet's congressional papers from when he was a senator, as well as Dellet family books. The original plantation sofa is stuffed with cotton from the fields. Candlesticks on the small table are Chinese Ming porcelain in the shape of rabbits. On the wall is an 1840 map of Paris showing Emma Dellet's different carriage routes. Once folded into a beautifully covered moiré book, it has now been framed. The border shows Paris's most important buildings, many of which were destroyed in the Franco-Prussian war. By one window is a modern telescope; by the other, antique globes.

The American Empire bed (LEFT) was part of the house's original furnishings. The mantel was carved on the plantation for the house. The sofa is French of the Napoleon III period and is part of a set (the rest is in another house in Mobile). Between the windows are lithographs from Diderot's Encyclopaedia *that show scenes of the Palais Royale when it belonged to the Duc d'Orléans.*

ily are still in the house today. These include volumes in Latin, French, German, and Italian, as well as first editions of William Makepeace Thackeray novels and, in the original paperbacks—because of their frailty, all the more rare—a set of Charles Dickens.

Kitchens were always set apart from the main house in southern plantation homes, mainly because of the danger of fire. At one time a covered wooden walkway joined the kitchen to the main house, but it has long since deteriorated. Prepared meals used to be brought on large tole trays to the back porch of the main house, then placed on a table that had three raised sides that protected the food from drafts.

The old kitchen building, still intact, consists of two large rooms and an immense walk-in fireplace that is made from huge blocks of limestone cut from the bluff of the river with wet saws. The old kitchen was still in use until 1950, but the present owner plans to turn the building into a guest house. One room will become a bedroom and the other a museum/kitchen/sitting room. The floor will be covered with hemp rugs, and long wooden benches will be upholstered to use as sofas or single beds. Over the mantel in the kitchen is a dinosaur bone that was dug out of the Alabama River one mile away from Dellet Park. Other relics in the kitchen include metal shells from Civil War guns, an oak table with chairs, and cabinets, all of which were part of the original furnishings.

"The great thing about the house," says the present owner, "is that you can't see it from the road. You have no idea it's there." He has lined the three-quarter-mile drive with a charming avenue of magnolias and dogwood. The original fence around the house had rotted to the ground, but enough existed to have it copied. He also installed a round center circle of posts and chains, which is filled with daffodils in the spring.

"We entertain a lot. My wife, who is French, and I like to think of new places to have meals. Sometimes we picnic by the fountain; sometimes we just recline in wicker chairs on the glassed-in back porch—one of the most comfortable and prettiest rooms in the house. But perhaps the most *special* place is the porch on the second floor. You get the feeling you are in a perfect little Greek temple, high in the air."

The original details of the house, which were painstakingly

The Marquis de Lafayette slept on this bed (ABOVE) on his last trip to America. The bed, together with a matching chest and a little pull-out trundle bed underneath, was ordered from New York specially for Dellet Park. By the window is a doll's house designed by the owner for his children and made by a local carpenter.

executed, are still in good order, from the dentils under the cornice to the tympanum attic windows. The shutters still work perfectly and are continually used to keep out unwanted morning light or lessen the heat from the scorching midday sun. This is remarkable, considering the house was built by an unskilled and unsophisticated labor force.

The owners, and indeed the neighborhood, are anything but unsophisticated now. Harper Lee, the author of *To Kill a Mockingbird*, was a local resident; Truman Capote came from the nearby town and was a member of a children's writing group in Mobile.

Yet, to escape from this world and contemplate others, Dellet Park has the answer, too. "Sometimes we take the telescope outside and just look at the stars. There are no lights from the town, and it feels as if you can reach out and touch them."

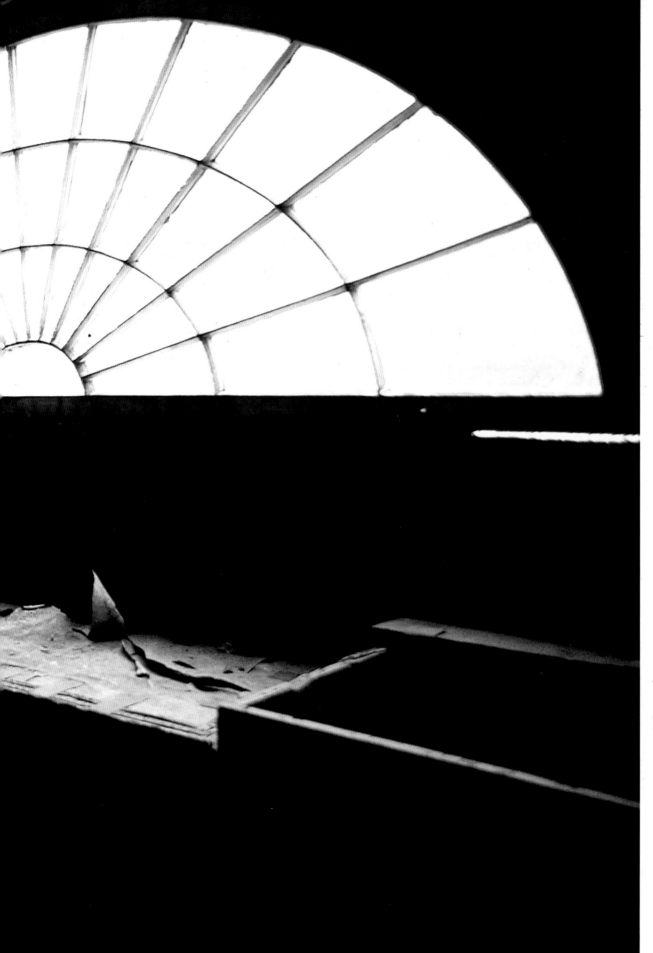

Tympanum windows were placed on either side of the attic story for ventilation. The zinc bath, on its mahogany stand, came from Paris and was used in the bathroom that was on the ground floor of the house. The builder of the house, Laurence Campbell, had been a master shipbuilder, and he used some of his previously learned skills constructing Dellet Park. For instance, the attic roof is constructed like a boat hull turned upside down.

131

THE CENTRAL STATES

The pioneers who pushed their way across North America in the nineteenth century were frequently those immigrants who had not established a satisfactory foothold on the East Coast. Younger, ambitious members of large families saw a stake in their future if they could establish their own plot of land on America's almost never-ending frontier. Irish, Scots, Finns, Dutchmen, Germans, and Scandinavians, along with Yankees and "Yorkies," headed to the West via the newly opened Erie Canal and the Great Lakes to clear the land, build houses, and plant wheat on the fresh, fertile soil.

Some of their farming practices were harmful and soon exhausted the rich earth, just as they had in the East. To adapt to a new kind of farming, as Mike Link in Journeys to Door County tells it, some turned to dairy farming. Looking after the family cows, which had almost been pets, previously had been the responsibility of the wives. It now became the farmers' work.

The feeding of vast numbers of cattle changed the shape of the farm complex with the invention of silage—from ensilage in French—to "keep cattle fodder succulent and nutritious." The Indians had dug pits for the storage of their corn, and the first farm silos were of a similar cellar type, but in 1873 Fred Hatch of McHenry County, Illinois, built a rectangular tower of heavy timber to store his green fodder. Later silos were built in stone or brick, and they gradually took on the circular shape that is familiar today. At first, many farmers resisted the idea of silage because it meant they were giving fermented food to their cattle. Some creameries refused to buy milk from cows that had been fed silage. According to Mike Link, in 1882 there were only ninety-one silos in the United States, but by 1923 the number had grown to 100,000. Nowadays silos are sheathed in silver-toned shingles or shiny blue tiles, and are recognized as an integral part of the farm landscape.

Early houses and barns in the Central states were often made of logs. The Finnish and Swedish settlers excelled at this kind of building, as they had a century earlier on the East Coast, and because log houses were part of their cultural heritage, they built them for permanence. The logs they cut from the heavily wooded forests were allowed to mature before being used, and they were hewn and fitted so closely that sometimes the only chinking needed was a strip of fabric between each log. The corners of these log houses were held by double notches or by the full dovetail notch, which required skill to execute but provided the firmest bind as Allen G. Noble states' in Wood, Brick & Stone.

Barns were frequently constructed from round or unhewn logs, and the upper parts where the hay was stored were left unchinked to allow ventilation. Log barns and houses, though often crude, could be erected relatively quickly and by few people; women could help by handling the ox- or horse-drawn wagons that brought the logs from the forests.

The log house has become a symbol for the rugged but virtuous rustic dwelling; many nineteenth-century politicians claimed a special blessing for having been born in one. Modern versions that pop up in suburbia are made from machine-smoothed logs shipped to the site by firms that specialize in their construction. However, very few of the old log houses, built out of necessity, still exist. From the 1850s onward, the wood-frame house dominated building construction.

According to Virginia and Lee McAlester in A Field Guide to American Houses, the balloon-frame system of construction, begun in Chicago in the 1830s, eliminated the need for tedious hewn and pegged joints and massive timbers of braced-frame and post-and-girt construction by joining standard-cut lumber with nails. Construction became cheaper and faster, and indeed, most houses in towns as well as rural areas were built by this method during the second half of the nineteenth century. In addition, house components—doors, windows, roofing, siding, and decorative detailing—began to be mass-produced in large factories and could be shipped at relatively low cost on the expanding complex of railways. Farmhouses, though simpler in style than most town dwellings, acquired fancy carved-wood trimming in what became the Victorian style—which embraced a variety of ornate details. Even the simple stone house at the Country Homestead (page 164) got its share of "gingerbread" trim on its porch, a concession to style more than function.

Styles in architecture were much discussed from the middle of the nineteenth century on. The most widely read books on the subject were by Andrew Jackson Downing (1815–1872) a failed landscape architect who became well known for two of his books, Cottage Residences (1842) and The Architecture of Country Houses (1850). He suggested designs for farmhouses, among other rural dwellings, showing plans and discussing their function, but his main theme was that the perception of beauty in buildings contributed to a great moral crusade. "Everything in architecture that could be made a symbol of social or domestic virtue added to its beauty and exalted it." This theme rang a bell with Americans, whose Constitution separated government from religion; the home had to be the place where all moral guidance started, in lieu of a state religion.

The agricultural press in America voiced some concern that Downing's designs were too elaborate for the average farmer who put all his efforts and resources into securing his crops and livestock. Despite this criticism, Downing's books were influential. The ordinary American became aware that the design and decoration of their own houses

136

could go beyond mere function and beyond the classical forms into the realms of the romantic and the picturesque.

Out of necessity, the earliest farmhouses were furnished with simple homemade essentials and the occasional family treasure—a Bible perhaps, or china, or brass candlesticks from back East or from Europe. However, as the nineteenth century progressed, mass-produced furniture became available. Factories sprang up near many of the major cities. In the Midwest, Grand Rapids, close to ample supplies of wood, became a center for inexpensively manufactured furniture. And by the 1860s, mail-order catalogs provided goods for all parts of the house at a variety of prices.

Nonetheless, the farmer's wife was responsible for the look of the interior of her house, whatever her budget. Though she could now purchase woolen goods by the yard instead of having to spin and weave it herself, she still made clothing for herself, her children, and often for her husband. Many garments and household linens such as drying cloths were made out of flour sacks and feed bags. Curtains, quilts, and rag rugs were all made by the women of the house, although a hand-turned or treadle sewing machine became available to speed up the work. Household chores were still backbreaking compared to nowadays, but gradually labor-saving devices became the norm. Kitchens became separate rooms with their own stove for cooking. Although many houses had pumps outside (see Ek Trädet, page 146), some kitchens were fitted with a sink and pump indoors.

Up until the 1920s, many of the farms were still very simple. Major changes did not happen until the advent of the combustion engine, the telephone, and the enormous influence that the general use of electricity imparted to all of North America.

EK TRÄDET

WOOL GATHERING IN
DOOR COUNTY, WISCONSIN

The flagpole (RIGHT) in the garden flies a Swedish flag along with the Stars and Stripes. Recently renewed shingles cover insulation of the main house's log structure and provide weatherproofing.

The barn at Ek Trädet (LEFT) is across a gravel courtyard from the log house. At one time, a bull was kept on the ground floor; later the barn was used to raise pheasants. Large sliding doors on either side allowed a hay cart to enter on one side and exit on the other. The double-hung and screened dormer windows added in the 1970s were designed to let in more light.

D oor County is a thumb of land in northeastern Wisconsin, having Green Bay to the warmer, western side, and Lake Michigan to the east. Every corner of this county is dotted with small dairy farm complexes, fields of black-and-white Holstein cows, fruit orchards, gambrel-roofed barns, towering silos, and practical, unpretentious farmhouses.

Archaeologists are still tracing Indian cultures that existed in the area that is now Wisconsin back to between 7,000 and 10,000 years ago. In more recent history, tribes that included Ojibwas, Winnebagos, and Potawatomis, fought over the territory and were pressured by French explorers and trappers. The French were, as told by Mike Link in *Journeys to Door County,* "exploiters of the resources, and they intended to change the Indian from user to consumer." In turn, the French were defeated by the Anglo-Americans, who allied themselves with the warlike Iroquois, using Indian against Indian. The Door County Indians who survived were finally faced with the pioneer farmers who started to arrive in the 1830s. In 1848 Wisconsin was admitted to the Union as the thirtieth state. By then very few outward signs of the long-lasting Indian presence remained.

Indeed, very few of the early buildings of the compar-

The entrance to the main selling area of the Ek Trädet store is through this door of the barn. The walkway is made from deck boards.

EK
TRÄDET

The main part of the house (ABOVE), built by August Dorn in 1880, is of horizontal log construction. The stovewood kitchen wing, by the rain barrel, was added around 1910. White and purple lilac trees around the house are about to blossom. Hanging baskets of fuchsia and pots of geraniums herald the all-too-brief summer season in Door County. The still-working, hand-operated lawn mower belonged to the owner's grandparents; the wooden chairs were fashioned by a local carpenter.

atively recent pioneers survive. Those that do exist are almost all log structures, which were typical of midwestern settlers who used the trees they cut down to build their dwellings as they cleared the land. Primitive frontier conditions existed in some parts of Wisconsin right up until the early twentieth century, and many log houses were still being built then.

The farmhouse that is now called Ek Trädet is between Bailey's Harbor and Sister Bay in Door County. The exact date it was built is not clear; according to architectural historian Richard W. E. Perrin in *Historic Wisconsin Buildings,* the farmstead was established around 1880; members of the Zachow family who were born in the house put the date at 1890; and John Kahlert, a recent owner and author of *Early Door County Buildings,* says it was 1895. The original house was built by August Dorn, from Pomerania. He was one of the earliest German settlers of the area and had already built a house for himself and his family on the opposite side of the road in 1860 before embarking on Ek Trädet. When he was well into his fifties, August Dorn built Ek Trädet for his daughter, Amalia, and her husband, a fellow Pomeranian named William Zachow.

The Zachow House, as it was then known, was built of horizontal log construction. The logs were square hewn, the preferred method, which gave flatter surfaces and made a tighter wall. The interstices were filled with mud or clay. The interior was plastered to give smooth inside walls and add status to the house. The outside was shingled, completely hiding the log construction. This served to weatherproof and insulate the house and preserved the chinking, which otherwise would have been dislodged by the harsh Wisconsin winters.

A barn with a masonry first floor was built to house the farm animals. A second floor of wood stored hay to feed them. As the farm grew, the barn was expanded. Bill Zachow, who

The front parlor, or music room (FAR LEFT), houses a turn-of-the-century Kimberly organ, bought in Chicago. The Moroccan wool carpet is modern. The grandfather clock in the corner is a modern reproduction made by Seboda and purchased in Wisconsin. A wall hanging made by Normajean Ek's mother is called a rya, which is a Swedish form of knotting. To the left of the clock is a watercolor of Door County painted by the owner. The American pine chest of drawers between the windows belonged to Normajean Ek's grandmother. The wall hanging between the windows and the woven wool cushions were all made by the owner.

Walls of the living room (LEFT) show the horizontal log construction, which had been covered with plaster until 1974, when the house was restored by then owner John Kahlert. In 1978, when Normajean Ek acquired the house, further renovations were made. The ceiling was opened up, exposing the beams, to give a lighter, brighter atmosphere to the room. Fire screens and doors were added to the fireplace, which had been part of the Kahlerts' restoration. Hanging from the rails on the floor above and giving some privacy to the bedroom are, from left to right: a blanket from Guatemala, a Mexican woven blanket, a quilt (made by a Wisconsin quilter whose work can be purchased at Ek Trädet), and a blue hanging made by the owner. The sheepskin in the foreground is from New Zealand.

The stovewood construction of the walls in this kitchen (BELOW), which was added to the original log house in 1910, can be clearly seen. The new flooring is of quarry tile, installed in 1978. A side table holding traditional English pudding basins was converted by Normajean Ek's father from her grandmother's treadle sewing machine table. Beneath the window is an old coffee grinder from an A & P supermarket. The shawl on the bentwood rocking chair belonged to Normajean Ek's grandmother.

When the kitchen wing was remodeled in 1978, a central island of cedar topped with butcher block of maple and cherry Door County wood was constructed and hand finished by Carlsville cabinetmaker Gary Orthober. This island incorporates drawers, cabinets, oven, countertop burners, garbage receptacle, and plenty of working counter space. The main source of heat comes from a Round Oak stove made in the 1890s, bought in a Chicago antique shop, and selected for its name—ek means oak in Swedish. A schoolroom clock made around 1910 hangs on the stovewood constructed wall. Above the round table in the corner, a simple Swedish chandelier holds candles that are frequently lit for the evening meal. The curtains were screen printed by Door County artist Carol Gresko Lyons, in a pattern called "Door County apples and ladders."

was born in the farmhouse, remembers this all-wood structure being built. In an article in *The Door County Advocate,* he says: "In a barn-raising bee, that was the day it went up, but the parts were made a good while before. It took different special skills to get it all together. The wood itself might have been felled by my Dad, and his brother and maybe some others. Probably got help, that was the custom. Enaway [sic] after they actually cut the wood, it had to be hewn. Now there was only a few who could do that. It was done with what we called a broad ax and a lumberman would get this broad ax, Augustus Johns, the barnbuilder was one, he lived in Fish Creek, and would walk down the length of a timber with that ax right next to his foot and split it. Didn't make too many wrong strokes, that's sure. Then another fellow would make the routes there for the holding pegs. They do that with machine now. No one even knows how to do it by hand, anymore. Then the whole thing, the main supports, were gradually assembled and 'raised' by a bunch of neighbors under the general instructions of the barnbuilder. He had the whole plan in his head. Then Father and us kids and his brother finished off the siding and the interior lofts." A pulley still remains inside the roof of the barn where Bill Zachow used to haul the hay up from the wagon to the loft.

One difference between the old part of the barn and the new is that part of the old section's second floor was made with a stovewood construction inside the vertical weatherboards. Stovewood construction was also used on a granary that until recently stood near the barn. Alas, all that remains of the granary is a pile of wood and a photograph by Richard W. E. Perrin in his article "Wisconsin's Stovewood Architecture" in the *Wisconsin Academy Review.*

Luckily, stovewood construction is well represented in the Zachow farmhouse. A wing using this technique was built onto the log structure in 1910. This addition was hardly surprising, for by then there were ten children in the Zachow family, and they all slept in the upstairs loft of the small farmhouse, although, as they tell it, they were never conscious of feeling cramped.

Stovewood construction is thought to have originated in Canada among the lumberjacks, who, according to Sibyl Moholy-Nagy, considered it usable only for temporary forms of shelter. Found more frequently in Wisconsin than in any other American state, and in Door County in particular, stovewood houses reached their peak of popularity around 1910.

The name *stovewood* is derived from the pieces of wood that are cut to a size to fit into a stove. Trunks of trees, branches, or split logs can be used. These are laid one on top of the other as for a woodpile, packed tightly and solidly bedded in lime mortar, forming a wall. Sometimes this technique is called woodblock masonry or cordwood construction, a cord being a measure of wood cut for fuel—128 cubic feet, or four by four by eight feet. Many stovewood houses have been built in the twentieth century. A handbook, *Cordwood Construc-*

Baskets of experimental crochet work or knitting can be found everywhere in the house, even the bedroom. In progress by the bed is a crocheted rug made of marine rope. Gary Orthober built the cedar closets during the 1978 renovation, when a partition was erected between the main bedroom and the small loft bedroom Sarah sleeps in. The rocking chair, circa 1880, is called a sewing rocking chair because, being armless, it leaves the arms free for working. Beyond it is a sewing box decorated with rosemaling, a curlicue form of painting in shaded colors requiring precise brushwork that originated in Norway. The quilt on the bed was worked by Chicago quilt maker Judy Walters. A humpbacked chest at the foot of the bed, made of pine early in the nineteenth century, was originally covered in heavy paper for decoration. Normajean Ek made the heart-shaped basket that is hanging from the ceiling. The lace cloth on the round table is of hand-crocheted cotton, found in an antique shop. The shading variations indicate it was probably made with yarns from different dye lots.

tion by Richard Flatau, became popular enough to require a second printing in 1984. In it the author describes in layman's terms how to build a stovewood house.

According to Perrin, there are two types of basic stovewood construction. One type, used mainly for barn construction, is of a massive nature, built without a frame and completely self-supporting. Corners are formed with squared timber blocks similar to the cut-stone quoins in rubble masonry walls. The walls might be from fourteen to twenty inches thick. A second type of construction was used for houses and required a braced frame of hewn timber with stovewood used as nogging, as if the cut pieces of wood were used as end-on bricks to fill up the spaces. The width of the framing timbers determined the length of the stovewood pieces. This could vary, but those on the Zachow farmhouse, which is constructed by this second method, are six-inch logs of cedar. Other woods can be used, such as tamarack (larch), locust, various pines, hemlock, balsam, spruce, oak, maple, beech, or ash.

Once the walls and roof of a house were in place, the exterior of the house would often be shingled, as was the Zachow farmhouse; clad with vertical boards, as was the Zachow barn; or clapboarded. This cladding would preserve the mortar. The interiors were often plastered. Most stovewood houses were only one story high due to the extremely solid weight of the walls.

The 1910 stovewood wing of the Zachow house was added as a kitchen. A glass-fronted cupboard built into the corner was used then, as now, to hold china and glasses. Wainscoting—vertical paneled wood—was added to the lower part of the interior walls.

There was still no running water in the house in 1910. Water had to be brought from a pump house, a building nearby that is still standing and used now as a storage shed. Minnie Zachow, one of the ten children, can remember that it was her job to fetch the water even on the bitterly cold days. "One time, when I was real little, it was so cold out, and I put my tongue on the pump handle. Well, it about stuck there. Scared me half to death and I never did that again!"

Not long after the kitchen was added, the Zachows moved to Fish Creek. According to John Kahlert, the property passed through several hands, being used mostly by migrant fruit pick-

Partitioned from the main bedroom is Sarah's room. Part of the second floor was removed in 1978 so that the living room below could have a high ceiling. This gives Sarah's room the effect of a loft. In the original house, when the second floor was intact, ten children slept on this one floor. Although Sarah's clippings and posters may change from month to month, many childhood toys remain constant. The doll's buggy is from Sweden. Stuffed sheep by the bed can be bought at Ek Trädet. The quilt and mattress cover are made from printed sheeting. A collection of hats belonged to Sarah's grandfather. The floor planks and ceiling beams were all part of the original house.

ers. For some thirty years, the house was entirely vacant. In 1968 it was acquired by Kenneth Delwiche of Green Bay, who began to restore the house, which by then had reached a point of almost irretrievable disrepair. His untimely death halted the project, and John Kahlert bought the house and its accompanying buildings and continued the restoration work. Prevailing taste in the second half of the twentieth century has been to reveal as much of the structure of a house as possible, so plaster that covered the log and stovewood walls was stripped, walls were bleached and sanded, and beams exposed. Restoration of the barn was begun by artists Richard and Claire Bierman. A cement floor was laid in the barn, windows were added to let in more light, and the roof and walls were repaired.

In 1978 the Zachow House acquired its new and present owner and also a new name—Ek Trädet, which means "the oak tree" in Swedish. Normajean Johnson Ek had been raised in Michigan and lived in Chicago. Of Swedish descent, she had spent many pleasant summer vacations in Door County and had often driven past the Zachow place, admiring the idyllic grouping of the buildings and their surrounding orchards. When she discovered it was for sale, she bought it and moved

This bathroom was installed downstairs as part of the 1978 renovation. Previous owners used an outhouse that was situated by the pear trees in the orchard, and water for washing came from an outdoor pump. Asked to make simple but rustic towel and toilet-paper holders, Gary Orthober invented the pegged fixtures that can be seen reflected in the mirror. A white towel embroidered with hearts bears the motto "May the wool of your sheep be long and warm," which was worked by a friend as a gift. The medicine cabinet is of generous proportions, and a narrow upright closet leads to a large storage area, which will be converted into a sauna in keeping with the Scandinavian character of the house.

The wood-constructed end of the barn is used partly as a selling area and partly for Ek Trädet's workshops (ABOVE AND RIGHT). Track lighting has been affixed to the rough beams, and electric heating under the cement floor can be augmented by a wood-burning stove on chilly days. A variety of looms to use in the workshops or to purchase are available, and Ek Tradët stocks a wide choice of natural-fiber yarns from all over the world.

An antique non-functional bathtub, found in Ephraim, Door County, is filled with cotton rugs handwoven by local artisans (FAR RIGHT). All-wool yarns, handmade baskets, and soap in the form of apples cajole the eye in this rough-plastered and whitewashed room.

in with her daughter, Sarah, and set about trying to fit the furniture from her eleven-room house in Chicago into the tiny log house.

Normajean Ek had a further motive behind the purchase. The spacious barn would make an ideal setting to sell what she terms "wearable art," and there would still be plenty of space to hold workshops for those interested in life-enrichment classes. Although there was much to be done to make the property viable for such an ambitious project, it was as if everything she had done in her life up to that point led to this goal.

Interested in knitting as a child, Normajean Ek majored in home economics at Michigan State University, studying art and business as well. After college she worked in retail and fashion-related jobs in Chicago. This experience and background "guided her in the creation of her boutique, which specializes in quality handmade garments, the fibers necessary to make garments, and instructions as to how to make them," as Pipka Ulvilden wrote in *The Best of Door County,* a useful resource book about the artists, shops, and eating places of the area. The shop has been so successful that a new boutique opened in 1986 in the Bailey's Harbor Yacht Club.

The Leisure Learning Workshops at Ek Trädet over the past eight years have included herb craft, weaving, pottery, solar-energy planning, seeing-drawing classes, bread sculpture, wild plant photography, tapestry making, Scandinavian folk dancing, poetry workshops, Zen and the art of writing, photographing Door County historic sites, basketry, knitting, felting, carding, spinning, dyeing, porcelain inlay, and fabric painting. In addition, Ek Trädet welcomes friends, neighbors, and customers to watch the farm's sheep being shorn—their wool goes into many of Ek Trädet's products—or the resident Angora rabbits being plucked.

To make the barn into a suitable place to sell clothing and to run workshops, Normajean Ek brought in electricity and added track lighting along the barn beams and wood-burning stoves and chimneys. Heating was installed under the cement floor, and an electrically operated, traditional compost, Swedish-style toilet was installed in a dressing room.

Major renovations took place in the farmhouse. A new contemporary environment was created in the kitchen, where a central cedar island, sinks, and work counters were installed. Also on the ground floor, a bathroom was constructed. In keeping with the Scandinavian character of the house, a sauna is to be added in what is now used as storage space near the present shower stall. Upstairs, part of the living room ceiling was removed, exposing beams and giving more loft to the room. The simple, farm-style, turn-of-the-century Swedish and American furniture mixes easily with contemporary and serviceable leather sofas and chairs.

The vintage barn and the old-fashioned log farmhouse of Ek Trädet are not, however, meant to signal a return to the past but to show the beauty and durability of things of value.

In Ek Trädet's orchard, the simple table and benches were designed and made by a local carpenter. The 1910 American bubbled blue pitcher and glasses belonged to the owner's grandmother. The farm's old orchard includes apple, pear, and cherry trees; chokecherry trees, which produce a wild, sour cherry that can be made into jam and wine; wild strawberries; asparagus that has escaped from its original bed and now grows wild all over the meadow; and morels, which are large, edible fungi for gourmet mushroom hunters.

FARAWAY RANCH
A LOG CABIN IN THE MOUNTAINS OF COLORADO

Elk antlers found on the ranch decorate a storage shed (LEFT) that is attached to the old log cabin.

Built in 1881 as a granary and bunkhouse, the log cabin (RIGHT) was moved from Aspen to its present spot in 1971. A Dutch door that leads from the kitchen enables Loey Ringquist to call her dogs without letting them into the house. To the right and back of the log cabin are a storage shed, a barn, an outhouse, and an area where the owner cuts and splits wood for her stoves. To the left of the houses are a vegetable garden and a chicken coop.

C olorado has the highest average elevation of all the North American states. Topped with snow for most of the year, the mountains can be seen for miles through the clear Colorado air. On the western slope, driving from Montrose through the San Miguel Canyon, there are huge red cliffs that have been fashioned by the elements over the centuries. In fact, the name Colorado is derived from the Spanish, meaning ruddy or red colored. An ear-popping climb from the San Miguel Canyon up onto the Norwood Mesa leads to Faraway Ranch, which consists of 2,000 acres of choice ranch land 7,000 feet above sea level.

The original Indians of the region, the Utes, were warriors from the plains who had been pushed over from the eastern slopes of Colorado to the western part of the state by the encroaching white men. Missionaries tried to teach them to be farmers, but husbandry was not in their nature and many rebelled. Gradually they were ousted by the settlers. A museum in Montrose is devoted to their culture, one of the few museums in the United States to be dedicated to a single tribe of American Indians.

Mining drew most of the earliest settlers to the state. It is believed that the triangle formed by Silverton, Ouray, and Tell-

uride has the richest mineral deposits in the world, although the last-named town gains its prosperity now from the ski trade. The world's largest silver nugget was produced in Aspen. In addition, gold, lead, zinc, and copper are found, and farther south are deposits of even more precious metals: vanadium (alloyed to other metals for strength and durability) and uranium (used in the production of plutonium for atomic energy). The mountains of the western slope once were dotted with mining camps, but nowadays mining is an expensive proposition and much of the industry has closed down.

Loey Ringquist, the owner of Faraway Ranch in southwestern Colorado, was born in Massachusetts, and her twin sister, Louise, lives close by. Their father was an inventor of gears for cars, and their mother was a legal secretary. Westminster, Massachusetts, the town of their birth, was badly hit by the Depression, so when their mother was offered a job in Yosemite National Park, California, the family moved west. The girls were only twelve, but Loey Ringquist can remember every day of the trip. They traveled by steamer for three weeks, through the Panama Canal and up the California coast. The whole journey cost $100 per adult and $75 for each child. They drove to Yosemite in the rumble seat of a Model A.

At first the girls felt hemmed in by the high mountains, but by the time they went to high school—forty-five miles each way—they had become accustomed to the scenery and felt right at home. The Conservation Corps—an organization that employed eighteen-year-old youths to care for the land—had just been started, and Loey Ringquist's father taught mechanics to them. After several moves, mostly to be close to schools, the girls went to Berkeley, and Loey Ringquist herself worked in Yosemite National Park. She became interested in photography after meeting Ansel Adams, who showed her unforgettable images of Colorado's magnificent landscape. For a while she worked with her sister and brother-in-law, who was a photographer, before setting off with a fellow photographer and a dancer in her own Model A for the Indian country of Colorado.

Aspen was just another town in the mountains after World War II. The men of the army's Tenth Mountain Division were learning warfare skiing at Leadville, across the hill, but as a sport skiing was in its infancy in the United States. New Hampshire had a ski trail, and there was one in California, but that was it until an entrepreneur opened a ski area in Aspen. Loey Ringquist heard they needed a photographer and joined them in their second season.

Dried grasses and mineral rocks share the hall table (LEFT).

Horseshoes found on the property form a decorative motif (RIGHT). *The scissor-shaped implement came from an old mine and was used for dragging logs.*

The right-hand side of this hallway (RIGHT) used to be the outside wall of the log cabin. Rough foundation rocks contrast with the smooth, purple, Vermont slate floors and form a rustic step up into the older building. Louise Gerdts, the owner's twin sister, made the wall hangings using rug remnants, odd pieces of jewelry, and findings from the fields or mining camps. The pink 1920s lamps came from a boarding house in Aspen.

The eating area (FAR RIGHT) in the newly renovated kitchen of the 1881 log cabin centers around a poker table that came from a gaming house called The Red Onion. A slot for poker chips is in the center of the table, which Loey Ringquist painted a vivid green. In her enthusiasm for bright colors, she painted the chairs around it blue. An accumulation of old and new household objects, useful and sentimental, decorates walls and shelves.

156

She had many interesting jobs during the years she lived in Aspen, but all of them related to her love of the outdoors and her interest in animals. She conducted jeep tours through the countryside; worked on the television show *Sergeant Preston of the Yukon,* assisting with the husky sled dogs; and, like many people lured to Colorado, did her share of prospecting.

Living in Aspen, Loey Rinquist had the wit to see that the ski business was a growing one. Predicting a boom, she found two partners, borrowed money from her mother, and bought a small ranch of 177 acres some ten miles from Aspen. This spot happened to be Snowmass.

There were three buildings on the property; the larger two went to her partners, and the smallest one, an old, broken-down, roofless log cabin, she fixed up for herself. Not only was the cabin filthy from livestock that had been allowed to wander through it, but over the years when it had been used as a family home, the owners, of which she was the fourth, had stuffed old rags and paper between the logs as insulation and nailed on a patchwork of flattened-out tin cans to hold the stuffing in place. She had to remove hundreds of nails from the interior walls, although the original logs had been so carefully dove-tailed at the corners they had not needed a single nail to keep them structurally in place. While removing the old insulation, she came across an 1881 newspaper, which helped to date the structure, and she was able to establish that the cabin had been built by a Tom Kearns.

On the rough walls of the living room (LEFT) hangs a Ute Indian lodge shield. Originally used for spiritual protection, it was traded for a sleigh in a Salt Lake City art gallery. Next to it is a hundred-year-old Indian bridle, and a piece of Indian-inspired needlepoint worked by a friend. Glass and porcelain telephone pole insulators are used as candle holders. The cane sofa came from the family home in Massachusetts. The foreground table is made from old foundry bellows supported by bricks.

The owner's nephew, Christopher Gerdts, put in the herringbone ceiling of weathered sheep corral boards (BELOW). Lance Hood, an Oklahoma Cherokee artist, painted the spiritual picture Warriors on the Plains in the 1930s. The blue lamp, below, was bought in Alaska by Loey Ringquist when she was twenty-two as a present for her mother. Shelves above the couch hold pottery and glass from New England. The rocking chair of willow was traded at Jack's Trading Post in exchange for a brass bed; the decorative dotted effect is formed by nicking off the bark at even intervals.

A *Fisher stove* (LEFT) *nestles under stairs of the old cabin, which lead to the sleeping alcove. The owner's father built the staircase from lodgepole pine—long, slender pines used for assembling Indian tepees. Old mining implements found on abandoned campsites, antique shoe lasts, favorite pictures, and an Indian serape decorate the walls.*

This living room (BELOW) is a part of the log house that was added in 1981, brought from the summer ranch on Wilson Mesa. The hundred-year-old aspen logs used were particularly tall and straight, being thirty-six-feet long and fifteen-inches wide. Woodworking tools on the wall under the stairs are from local antiques shops. Under the window is an old incubator that used to be run by kerosene. Its red color was exactly duplicated for the ceiling beams.

As property values soared around Snowmass, Loey Ring-quist organized the sale of her share. A complicated exchange involving five lawyers, thirteen people, and split-second timing was finalized one blizzardy New Year's Eve. When the deal was consummated, she had exchanged thirty-three acres in Snow-mass for 2,000 acres in Norwood. "They didn't much like a woman getting the prettiest piece of land in these parts," she remembers. Finding it hard to get reliable ranch hands, the owner did most of the work herself. She had to prevent her livestock from eating frozen vegetation in the winter and main-tain the essential irrigation system that Colorado's dry summer climate demands. After years of working to the limits of her strength, she decided to lease out portions of her land to other ranchers.

When the land exchange from Snowmass to Norwood took place, Loey Ringquist had permission to move her log cabin home to Faraway Ranch, the name for her new property. In the summer of 1971, a crane pulled the peaks of the cabin apart and laid the roof down so that the old cabin resembled "a huge, decrepit matchbox," as she described it.

Typically, a ranch in the western part of Colorado has a "home place" down low where hay, alfalfa, and oats can be grown for the livestock and where the animals can spend the winter, and another camp higher up for beneficial summer grazing, where the grass is high in nutrients and the worms and flies are at a minimum. Loey Ringquist's purchase included a "summer ranch" on Wilson Mesa, thirty-five miles up the San Miguel Canyon and fifteen miles southwest of Telluride. This mesa is 9,500 feet high and surrounded by the rim of the Rock-ies. On the mesa was an old ranch house to which a log home-steader cabin was joined. By removing the roof, which had

rotted, and cleaning out all the debris that had accumulated over the past fifty years, Loey Ringquist felt she could disman-tle the log cabin and join it to her cabin, now settled in Nor-wood. The logs of this homestead cabin were unusually long—sixteen feet—and of aspen. They were laid out to "sun" for ten years before she felt they could be used in rebuilding the dwelling.

In exchange for moving the logs down from Wilson Mesa and putting up the basic structure, Loey Ringquist traded a down payment on a piece of land to three young men—two contractor-carpenters and a stonemason. The old cabin was rebuilt alongside the log house from Snowmass so that the out-side wall of the Snowmass cabin was enclosed inside, forming a hallway. The rough fieldstone foundation formed a step be-cause the two houses are on slightly different levels. The stone-mason laid the new foundations and put in new floors of

The master bedroom (FAR LEFT) in the 1980 house looks out over the ranchlands on a plateau 7,000 feet above sea level. The bed, from Maine, had four layers of paint that the owner's father painstakingly removed. The cat picture in the far corner was found in an old nearby building, and Louise Gerdts made the fur frame for it. Pieces of antique china from Massachusetts and a collection of shells cohabit the shelf below.

The sleeping loft (LEFT) within the sloping beams of the roof can just accommodate two people. The overhead fabric, a lap robe for a sleigh, is a hundred years old. It works well against the deep color of the untreated beams and adds warmth and protection from bumping one's head.

In addition to the emergency outhouse, the 1980 house includes a bathroom with shower and tub (RIGHT). A tiny Upland stove heats the room in minutes. Logs are stored in an alcove under the washbasin. A hall stand—chair, mirror, and coat hooks—is used to hold towels.

161

Vermont slate. Additional lumber was gleaned from an old sheep homestead that was on her sister's property. For a couple of years prior to the log cabin addition, the owner had been tearing the sheep sheds apart and storing the old wood, which was eventually used for the siding. The inside beams came from the sheep shed roofs, and decorative inside trim came from the sheep corrals, or fences. The stairs in the new addition came from an old weighing station brought from nearby Placerville by a former rancher. The rails on the stair's banister came from a hay bucker that had been left in a field. Hay buckers stacked loose hay into either a barn or into a big stack; a team of horses would be used to pull the newly made stack onto a rack that propelled the stack up onto the old stack or into the loft or barn.

This addition took place in 1980. At the same time, a large storeroom was included and a new, roomy bathroom. The local water is fine to use for washing but contains too many harmful minerals to be good to drink, so drinking water has to be brought in by bottle. A complete basement and good insulation were also part of the installation.

The two houses joined together now consist of two living rooms downstairs (one can double as a bedroom), a hallway, a storage room, and a large, newly renovated kitchen. This kitchen was completely remodeled in 1985 when a local carpenter-contractor built in new cupboards, counter space, sink, and refrigerator. Vinyl floor covering in a tile motif covers the wood floor. A wooden deck surrounds most of the house.

Upstairs are three bedrooms; one small bedroom is tucked under the eaves of the first house, and two larger bedrooms are reached by the staircase in the second house.

Throughout both houses is a much-loved, charmingly artless accumulation of favorite things: unframed pictures cut from calendars or catalogs and thumbtacked to the rough log walls; plants being nursed to health or seedling tomatoes brought in for the night; family treasures from the Massachusetts days, including six trunks of china as yet unpacked in the basement; groups of geological specimens clustered on desks and cabinets; animal horns found in the fields; interestingly shaped or grained pieces of wood; time-blackened mining paraphernalia garnered from old campsites; Indian artifacts, blankets, serapes, and bridles. In true farmhouse tradition, every object has a story and a reason for being there, and the effect is refreshingly unpretentious. Faraway Ranch is a dwelling made of natural materials: wood, stone, and earth.

Outside, behind the house, are a storage shed, a barn, and an outhouse that is used as a backup for the bathroom. In the summer a profusion of flowers surrounds the decks of the house, and a large garden supplies vegetables. Farther away is a chicken house where Aracuna hens from South America lay pale green eggs. Throughout the garden, Loey Ringquist's family of a dozen assorted dogs and four cats roam. Horses graze nearby. Beyond them all is a rim of distant mountains.

162

Faraway Ranch is situated on a mesa rimmed by mountains that remain snowcapped until July.

THE COUNTRY HOMESTEAD

A GERMAN ROCK FARMHOUSE NEAR
FREDERICKSBURG, TEXAS

A sixty-foot rock-lined well (RIGHT) *was discovered on the property. Originally flush with the ground, a circular enclosure was built over it and it was topped with an old wooden cover. It pays to be cautious opening it; scorpions are apt to lurk beneath.*

Fancy gingerbread trimming decorates the porch of the main rock house (LEFT), *which was built by William Kusenberger in the late 1870s. The house still has the original doors of hand-pegged cypress.*

Seventy miles west of Austin, past grass verges strewn with bluebonnets, the state flower of Texas, lies the town of Fredericksburg. This town was founded in 1846 by German immigrants. The German influence is unmistakable, from the names of families to the distinctive design of the early architecture.

The Country Homestead, in the Rocky Hill district, some six miles outside Fredericksburg, is a group of farm buildings set in the middle of rolling farmland. According to *Historic Homes In And Around Fredericksburg* by Elise Kowert, the land surrounding the homestead once belonged to a famed Texas ranger, John Coffee (Jack) Hays, who came from Tennessee to join the Texas army after the Battle of San Jacinto in 1836. He was also a courageous land surveyor who had a number of skirmishes with the Texas Indians, for whom the Spanish had named the region in 1528.

In 1840 Hays surveyed one-third of a league—1,476 acres—of land claimed by a certain J. D. Watkins. The claim was based on the fact that the Republic of Texas had declared its independence in September 1836, and any single man who was seventeen or older at that time was entitled to receive a third of a league of land. Hays must have liked the look of the piece he surveyed, for later he acquired the Watkins claim.

The present owner, Brenda Klein Speight, lives with her young son, Dan, in this renovated two-story horse barn. Grain was stored on the top floor of the original barn, and oats still occasionally fall through the floorboards. Unusual in this area where most of the horse barns are made of wood, three of the walls are of finely worked limestone rocks with tiny slots that let in light and ventilation. On ground level, the south side was originally open but has now been faced with vertical oak and cedar boards and a screened door. A goat cart made from old wood stands next to a flower-planted tub.

Hays sold his land in Texas when he moved to San Francisco to become sheriff and later surveyor general of California.

In 1872 the land was bought by Christian Kusenberger and Lorenz Schmidt. They paid $1,850 cash for the 1,476 acres and divided it into three tracts of almost equal size. Kusenberger got the western third. Born in 1826 in the dukedom of Nassau in Germany, he had become an American citizen in 1854. He married Catherine Weiershausen, whose family owned land nearby, and they had two sons, William and Louis, and three daughters, Pauline, Mina, and Christine. William married Pauline Koennecke in 1878, and they made their home on land given him by his parents, which consisted of the north 475½ acres of the Kusenberger land tract. The rest went to his brother, Louis, but both had to promise not to sell any part of the land in their parents' lifetime except to a sibling. It was William and Pauline Kusenberger who erected the complex of buildings that forms the Country Homestead.

The town of Fredericksburg nearby produced a unique style of dwelling known as the Sunday house. Only one still exists in its original state, which is the Weaver House on the grounds of the Pioneer Museum. Sunday houses were by no means the first houses in the town. The settlers' immediate concern was to provide shelter for themselves and their families, and so they erected crude brush huts as temporary shelters on their outlying ranch lands. Later came more permanent log cabins and *fachwerk* houses in which oak timbers were filled in with stone or brick and frequently the bricks were covered with plaster or whitewash. The stone house, or rock house

A swimming pool (ABOVE LEFT) was constructed by a firm that specializes in water tanks for cattle. The reinforced concrete tank was poured in three days and later faced by the owner with hewn limestone rocks that came from a tumbledown old house that she bought for the purpose. The inside of the filtered pool was painted dark to give the appearance of a natural, spring-fed pond. The lounging chairs under the trees are of bent willow made by a local craftsman.

The tree house (ABOVE RIGHT) was built from split cedar logs that had once been fences on the property. The rough-edged bark was used to make plank doors and shutters that can be fastened with forged hooks, and straplinger; the house also boasts electric lights and a shingle roof. A queen-size mattress just fits into the floor space for sleep-outs. Others may be accommodated on the platform porch.

A three-legged windmill (ABOVE) fills the cypress wood tank, which is balanced on cedar supports. The pump house is constructed like a log cabin. Through the native cedar trees (correctly called junipers) can be glimpsed the porch of the big rock house.

167

Beaded pine covers the kitchen cupboards, and cypress forms the sink surround (LEFT). Post oak, cedar, and red pine were used in the restoration, but the original hand- pegged beams and braces were used wherever possible. Plumbing pipes and electrical wires are hidden in hollowed-out ceiling beams. The old-fashioned cooking stove, Country Charm by House of Webster in Arkansas, is completely modern, efficient, and electric. The long dining room table in the foreground came from Taylor, Texas, where the owner's grandfather, Elmer Linville, used it in his workshop.

Believed to have been built in 1876, this pioneer house has tiny slits in the rock walls which provide just enough light and ventilation (RIGHT). A dry sink to the right holds a hand-appliquéd towel that belonged to the owner's grandmother. Blue-and-white breakfast bowls sit on patchwork table mats that are actually quilts for dolls' beds.

The ground floor of the rock-built barn forms a one-room living space that includes dining area and kitchen. Amish patchwork quilts cover the sofa, on which an original doll designed by the owner's sister, Judi Tasch, sits. Black mammy dolls holding hearts spill from the basket above. On the bench, a heart-shaped limestone rock is surrounded by naturally formed heart-shaped stones collected by young Dan. The pine used for the floorboards came from a local barn that was being demolished. The large cupboard to the right covered in beaded pine conceals stacked washing and drying machines, while the side facing the center of the room hides shelves of canned goods and condiments. The whole area can be heated on chilly days by the wood-burning stove or cooled during humid Texas summers by the ceiling fan.

as it is called in Texas, followed, and there are many of these still in existence in and around Fredericksburg.

In the late nineteenth and early twentieth centuries, small stone or timber houses were erected in the town initially for the farmers who lived so far away that a trip to town had to be an overnight event. They would attend to marketing on Saturday, perhaps go to a dance in the evening, to church on Sunday, and drive back to their ranch lands on Sunday night. Sunday houses had only one or two rooms, with a sleeping space above that was reached by an outside staircase. In time these houses grew as they became year-round residences for the older members of the family or for younger, enlarged families. Although Sunday houses are picturesque phenomena of Fredericksburg, the Country Homestead is older, more varied, and just as firmly rooted in the German tradition.

The entrance to the Country Homestead's driveway is marked by distinctive cedar posts and gates, held by a traditional hinge made of forked branches. This is the work of Arthur Sagebiel, a craftsman-contractor who has restored much of the Country Homestead. The one-and-a-half-mile drive winds through native post oaks, live oaks, and cedars (juniper trees), crossing over a wooden plank bridge. The ground cover is punctuated with cactus.

It is believed that the first structure built on the property is the wood barn, which has limestone rock rooms at either end. A corncrib, built of logs with the bark still on some of them, sits in the middle of this barn. One of the rock rooms was used to store cottonseed. Later other wooden sheds were added and used to store farm implements.

The first house on the farm was also built of limestone rock, supposedly in 1876, but this date is not documented anywhere. This house has only two rooms with a large root cellar beneath, but this was not an unusual arrangement, because many of the activities that might have taken place inside a house in a colder climate, such as Germany or that German hearth, Pennsylvania, could be accomplished outdoors in the warm weather of Texas. Great skill was used on the masonry in the house. Above the windows, front door, and even above the entrance to the cellar there are well-made keystone rock arches. One of the rooms later became a smokehouse after a new family house was built, and on the outside of this smoke room there is a waist-high rock enclosure that would have held a fire with a stone chimney against the side of the house. Water would have been heated in a black iron pot and used for washing and butchering the hogs.

After a few years a larger rock house was built some

Limestone walls contrast with wooden eaves in the master bedroom of the barn. The unusually large braided rug was found in Fredericksburg. The chest at the foot of the bed was bought in Dallas and is probably German. On it is an Amish quilt. All but one of the teddy bears in the old wooden cradle are modern reproductions.

A settle (ABOVE) *from Pennsylvania holds a collection of dolls manufactured by Judi Tasch. A wooden pitchfork behind the settle came from Spain. The sampler on the wall is a muslin bag with* The Country Sampler *logo. This was stitched originally by Brenda Klein Speight's mother as a birthday gift for her daughter; muslin bags of various sizes are printed with this design and used as wrapping bags in the store.*

This pine set of shelves from Ireland (RIGHT) would have been kept in a passage leading to the kitchen. The barred bottom shelf was used to hold chickens. Now the shelves are filled with folk art toys, old and new. Many of them, such as the paper-covered heart-shaped boxes, necklaces formed from tiny dolls, teddy bears, rabbits, and the hand-carved Noah's ark are all from The Country Sampler *in Fredericksburg.*

twenty yards away to accommodate the growing Kusenberger family. This dwelling consisted of four rooms and a hall at first, but later a wood-frame construction was added where the Kusenberger grandchildren, Edwin and Walter, slept. The second floor, reached by indoor and outdoor stairways, was used only for storage. Recently the indoor stairway was removed and moved to a large rock barn where it has been reconstructed to convert the barn into a residence for the present owner and her son. Both the big house and the barn have impressive stonework that was done by a local bachelor mason named John Richard, who was known for his skill in building stone barns in the area; it is also probable that Lorenz Schmidt, who shared the original tract of land with Christian Kusenberger, worked on the first pioneer house, because he too was a stonemason.

Of all the buildings in the compound, the large two-story horse barn is the most impressive. Three of its walls are of thick, cut limestone. The structure has been completely renovated by the nonstop energy and artistic judgment of Brenda Klein Speight, who acquired the property in 1979.

Inside the barn, both floors are packed with a pleasing mélange of old and new folk art, much of it being pieces that are presently on sale at the owner's two shops in Fredericksburg: The Country Sampler and The Settlers' House. The barn is a perfect showplace for her display talents, as well as being a comfortable home.

Other outbuildings abound. A horse barn has been completely restored. A swimming pool has been constructed like a cattle watering tank. The original well has been discovered and improved. The guard dog has been given his own log cabin kennel. Brenda Speight's son, Dan, has a tree house.

Next on the agenda is to convert the two-room pioneer house into a most desirable and comfortable bed-and-breakfast *gasthaus*, not to mention renovating the larger rock house, building a bathroom onto it, fixing the outside stairs, restoring the gingerbread carvings, and generally bringing the building back to life.

Indeed, bringing buildings back to life is what the Country Homestead is all about. Restoring them with care and attention, using the skills of today but with an appreciation of past craftsmanship, and enjoying the warmth and comfort of a German farmhouse built of local rocks or constructed from local trees—that is the message of this ranch and its reason for being.

An American brass bed with bandanna sheets fills this bedroom under the eaves. A Depression quilt at the foot of the bed is appliquéd with airplanes.

Waddles, a new duckling, takes a bath in a tub tucked under the eaves of the barn. The chest of drawers in the foreground belonged to the owner's grandmother. A polished wood, beautifully articulated hand used to show gloves or jewelry was given to Mrs. Speight when she worked in the Neiman-Marcus display department in Dallas. The wire-backed chair is one of a set of children's ice cream chairs and table.

The root cellar in the pioneer house is reached by steps leading from a trapdoor on the porch. The masonry has been meticulously worked even in this storeroom, which has niches for storing milk and dairy products. The floor of tamped earth is so hard it can be broom swept.

The earliest dwelling to be built on this homestead was the pioneer house (RIGHT). On the porch, a painted wheelbarrow from Pennsylvania holds wooden pumpkins and a watermelon made from a telephone pole.

THE WEST COAST

*T*he first Europeans to reach what is now California were the Spanish. Missionaries had built settlements in Baja California as early as 1697, but Upper California was ignored until 1769, when an expedition of Franciscan missionaries reached San Diego and established a mission. In 1770 another mission was established at Monterey. By 1832 nineteen additional missions had been founded, converting more than 80,000 Indians to Roman Catholicism. The missions developed into extensive plantations on which large herds of cattle were raised and rich crops of oranges, wheat, and olives were produced. California had been designated a province of Spain in 1804, but twenty years later it became part of the newly established Mexican Republic.

Many buildings in California were made of adobe, a Spanish-American name for a brick made of earth and hardened by exposure to the sun. The soil in California, being composed of quartz, clay, and other minerals in an extreme state of fineness, was

particularly suitable for making adobe bricks, which took from one to two weeks to bake and had to be turned every day. The process was not new—bricks made of clay mixed with straw had been used in ancient Egypt, Assyria, and Babylonia—but adobe bricks can be used only in regions with a limited rainfall. Most of California had the right climate for such building material.

The first American wagon train trekking from the east entered the province in 1826. For the next twenty years, California was torn by anticlericalism, separatism, dissatisfaction with Mexican rule, and demands for the secularization of the missions. Between 1835 and 1840, the missions were secularized and large tracts of land were taken over by ranchers. California became part of the United States in 1850. Many more European Americans poured into the state when gold was discovered at Sutter's Mill near Coloma, but most of the newcomers were unmarried men, including criminals, who wanted to get rich quick. Only ten percent of the population were women.

Reckless speculation, loose living, and lawless behavior were common in many localities. Houses, lacking the female influence, were rough and ready.

After the Civil War, when California was on the Union side, the state grew rapidly due to the completion of the Union Pacific Railroad. Trade and population increased. Chinese immigrants poured in to provide labor for the railways and the mines. By 1875 San Francisco had a population of about 200,000, including one hundred millionaires. And, of course, there was a lot of building.

In the last quarter of the nineteenth century, a conflict developed between the mining and the agricultural interests over the damage to the soil and water resources of the state caused by hydraulic mining methods. The issue was settled in favor of the farmers in 1884, and from then on agriculture became increasingly important to the economy of California.

Many of the ranchers' houses that had started as simple adobe dwellings in the 1840s took on more grandeur as the fortunes of the families increased. The original ranch house of Santa Clara del Norte (page 218) was a one-story adobe house. In Alexander Valley Vineyards, Cyrus Alexander's first house, still standing, was built of adobe bricks (page 184). By the time the California settlers were ready to expand their dwellings in the second half of the century, the balloon-frame system of building had become widespread. The further development of the platform, or Western frame, in which each story is erected as a separate unit, enabled stories to be added onto existing houses, as at Rancho Santa Clara del Norte, or new and elaborate houses to be erected from the ground up, as at Piedra Blanca Rancho (page 208). California provided forests of softwood trees that were suitable for making into lumber: redwood, yellow pine,

spruce, cedar, fir, and hemlock. Nails, necessary for balloon or platform framing, were now made from thin rods of steel and manufactured in large quantities instead of being hand-forged.

The Gothic Revival house was admirably suited for lumber construction. By the time the California ranchers were ready to improve their homes, they had been influenced by this style, which started as a conscious attempt to recall the Christianity of the Middle Ages. The effect is less aristocratic than the Greek Revival house, but more middle class and respectable. The Italianate house, following the Gothic Revival, had the cultural plus of implying a connection with the Italian Renaissance. Carved wooden details, brackets set under the roof, square cupolas crowning the roof, fancy balustrades on the porches, and trellises ventilating the cellar space below were all added to ranch houses. Frequently the houses were referred to as Victorian, after Britain's Queen Victoria, who reigned from 1837 to 1901, but the term is general and the styles of this period, whether borrowed from the medieval, the Renaissance, or the classical, all overlapped, sometimes to the extent that motifs from all three might be used on one house.

As the ranch houses took on importance, so did their interiors. In The American Home, Handlin tells us: "Before the Civil War it was assumed that the cultured and wealthy understood what constituted taste in home furnishing. That subject was part of their upbringing and education. If they needed advice, they had the connections and resources to obtain it. They consulted architects or skilled craftsmen who designed their homes and advised them about where to buy or who could make what furniture. . . . By the late 1860s discussions about good and bad taste were more common. The problem then was not how to find information but how to choose among conflicting opinions. Taste to many designers and critics was largely synonymous with ornament. They pointed out the significant features of different styles of furniture and told what principles to use to coordinate the colors and materials of the walls, floors and ceilings of a room. But what distinguished all of them was that they did not appear homemade. Through their detailing, material, and ornament such furniture and furnishings were overtly produced by skilled workers and appeared to be worth what they cost."

Rooms no longer were assembled by a process of accretion but could be furnished in suites, with every piece coordinated, bought at the same time. This was when family treasures, if any had made it to the West Coast, were relegated to attics. And because advice was available on what to buy, rather than how to make furniture, little was known about quality and craftsmanship in an age when manufacturers were seeking mass-produced shortcuts for their products, which might be at best naive and at worst gaudy.

California was, more than any other state, filled with uprooted people, "communities of well-to-do people, detached from the familiar European orientation and brought up against the unfamiliar Orient and embedded in a genial climate and exotic landscape," as Fitch wrote in American Building. The wide variety of its immigrants made for a variety of tastes. Although a respectable sobriety ruled in the wealthier settlements, West Coast taste in general seemed slightly shocking, unruly, a little too Spanish perhaps, and definitely not Anglo-Saxon. Those who had moved West to this kinder climate were happy not to put up with the stilted routines associated with the East Coast and New England. But, according to Handlin, "because they also did not want to appear uncultured they sometimes organized their houses more rigidly than the people who supposedly represented propriety and tradition." Traits of this kind can be observed in California ranch houses, which were shaped by conflicting impulses and lacked the coherence of more settled societies.

Some ranch houses, like southern plantation houses, were built with sumptuous proportions, in complete contrast to the small log cabins of the Midwest or the family farmhouses of the East. The entrance hall at Rancho Santa Clara del Norte is as big as a ballroom, and yet, to quote the American Agriculturalist in 1866, "The Hall is generally a mere passage-way to something better beyond and therefore it should not be so embellished as to attract special notice." One gets the impression that the wealthy Californians enjoyed revealing their affluence.

The balmy climate of the West Coast led to a new, more relaxed way of life, which in turn affected the dwellings. Fuel for warmth was not so essential, nor did houses have to be insulated. There was plenty of land, so houses could spread out and rooms could be higher and windows larger. Breezeways and patios became part of house designs. Fountains, pools, and irrigation systems were incorporated into gardens, along with luscious vegetation and, in southern California, the essential palm trees. Because they are less tied by traditions as a whole—although there are California families that go back to the early Spanish settlers—Californians are ready to embrace new ideas in the decoration of their houses. But each owner or custodian of these farmhouses has reinstalled or preserved furniture, mementos, and artifacts from the past while delighting in California's present.

ALEXANDER VALLEY VINEYARDS

A PIONEER HOMESTEAD
ON CALIFORNIA'S RUSSIAN RIVER

Spring gardens bloom in the re-established and enlarged gardens of Alexander Valley Vineyards (LEFT).

When the Wetzels first bought the Alexander Valley Vineyards, they decided to make this Victorian house (RIGHT) into a summer home for the family. In a state of disrepair, the house was taken apart, a new foundation poured, modern plumbing and wiring added, and the whole structure reassembled. The original redwood siding, carved gingerbread trimming, and original door and window frames were carefully saved, while seven coats of paint were removed from each.

In 1962 Harry and Margaret Wetzel started looking for a summer and weekend retreat on a river. After several transfers around the United States, the Wetzels settled in Los Angeles, but they wanted to put down roots in a more rural area. Friend and neighbor Russell Green led them to Healdsburg, on the Russian River, and persuaded them to go into partnership to develop the land as vineyards. For the last twenty years, this is what they have been doing.

The property the Wetzels purchased included a rundown 1848 Victorian house with a boarded-up front porch, surrounded by waist-high weeds, rubbish, and barbed wire. It had been neglected for years and apparently was altered during the Depression to house boarders, and the Wetzels wondered whether to fix it up or burn it down. Fortunately, Healdsburg's historian, Edwin Langhardt, visited them during their first summer there and told Maggie Wetzel the history of the house. Learning that the dilapidated structure had been built by the founder of Alexander Valley, Cyrus Alexander, she became determined to preserve the house and its surrounding grounds as well and as accurately as possible.

The founder's story is told by Charles Alexander in *The Life and Times of Cyrus Alexander*. Cyrus Alexander, called Aleck, was born on May 5, 1805, into a large Pennsylvania farm

family. He was a sickly child who spent most of his early years reading travel and adventure stories. As a young man he set off, at first to Illinois, to seek his fortune in mining; not finding success, he then joined the fur trade between St. Louis and the Far West. The hard life toughened him, although he lost his profits twice.

Undeterred, he headed for the Pacific Coast and, in San Diego, made friends with a wealthy trader, shipowner, and owner of large land holdings in Mexico, Captain Henry D. Fitch. Hearing rumors of good grazing land north of San Francisco, Fitch proposed that Alexander scout the area and report back. On the young man's recommendation, the Captain bought from the Mexican government eleven Spanish leagues called the Sotoyome grant, which was the equivalent of 48,000 acres. Fitch stocked the land with horses and cattle that Alexander was to guard and care for, taking as his share half the stock increase each year and the promise of two leagues, or 9,000 acres, at the end of his contract. Finally settled in one place, Alexander built a house. Helped by Digger Indians, he constructed an adobe dwelling made of sun-dried bricks cut from the soil. This first structure, built in 1841, has been restored by the Wetzels and stands near the main house.

Alexander procured implements and supplies from the closest town, Sonoma, thirty-five miles to the south. He planted an orchard, sowed wheat, and cleared the land of grizzly bears, panthers, coyotes, and wildcats. Gradually he began to meet his neighbors, all some distance away. One was a Mr. Gorden, who lived to the north at Cache Creek. His Spanish-Mexican wife had a sister who was a young woman just entering her teens. Cyrus Alexander began courting Rufena Lucerne, and they were married in December 1844.

Alexander built his last and grandest house as their residence in 1848. It had an adobe first floor and a redwood second story. The first-built adobe structure was relegated to being a separate kitchen. Later, tremors resulting from the San Francisco earthquake of 1906 destroyed the adobe first floor of the main house, and after the rubble was cleared, the second story was made into the first floor. It is this house, rebuilt and restored, that is the main house on the present-day vineyard.

By 1849 Californians had freed themselves from Mexican rule, and in 1850 California was admitted to the Union. Gold had been found at Sutter's Mill, and soon the valleys were overrun with miners. This created a market for meat, fruit, and vegetables. Fencing and irrigating his land, Alexander planted

An ancient wisteria vine climbs to the overhang of this 1841 adobe house (TOP), *the first dwelling built by Cyrus Alexander.*

The modern winery (LEFT) *is run by Harry Wetzel II, wine maker and general manager of Alexander Valley Vineyards. He created a naturally cooled cellar dug into the hillside, and designed a layout utilizing gravity for grape and wine movement.*

The new Sonoma barn is in a style peculiar to this part of the country and was built by local barn builders. Hay or grain is stored in the loft, while animals—in this case, sheep and chickens—are penned on either side of the central area on the ground floor.

This schoolhouse, which was built by Cyrus Alexander in 1868, used to be half a mile away from the main house, farther down the valley. Discovering that it was being used to store hay, Maggie Wetzel persuaded the owner, Lydia Goodyear, her neighbor, to sell it and allow the Wetzels to preserve another piece of history. The family poured a foundation on a scenic hilltop just above the Victorian house and moved the structure, meticulously restoring it in the process. Now a guest house, its single room is filled with period furniture.

grapevines, apples, and peaches. He founded a tannery to manufacture shoes and clothing, built and ran the first mill in the Russian River Valley, and made the first brick kiln in the county. At a time long before the advent of threshing machines, his method of threshing wheat was simply to pile the grain in a corral, drive in wild horses, and chase them around until the wheat was a mass of grain and chaff. The mass would be thrown in the air with a fork, and the wind would separate it from the grain.

By the 1850s new immigrants coming to the valley thought that Cyrus Alexander had more acreage than he needed. They began to squat on his land, as they already had at other California ranches. Finding that they wanted the land and were prepared to pay for it, Alexander hired surveyors and began to sell lots.

Now a wealthy and respected patriarch, he turned to religion and education. In California books were scarce. He ordered a Bible and returned to his boyhood hobby of reading. He

and his family built a church in the valley in the 1850s and later, in 1868, a schoolhouse. This last structure, which provided education for the people in the valley right up to the 1930s, was eventually discontinued as a school and used for storing hay. Maggie Wetzel persuaded the owner to sell it. Between 1970 and 1972, the Wetzels moved it from the valley to a hilltop overlooking the main house. Carefully restored, it is now used as a place for visiting family and friends.

Cyrus Alexander died in 1872, and his wife, Rufena, in 1908. They are both buried in the family cemetery on the Alexander Valley Vineyard's land. Their son, Tom, planted the gardens and built the low stone walls and ponds that are still in place today. His wife, Annie, lived on until the early 1960s, when the Alexander heirs sold the property to the Wetzels.

The first year that the Wetzels owned the main house, they and their children slept in sleeping bags on army cots and worked on the basics. They dug a well and installed a septic system, removed boards that had formed small, dark rooms,

186

In the schoolhouse sleeping gallery (RIGHT), two turn-of-the-century American brass beds are covered with simple navy-and-white quilts made by Laura Diggs. The original redwood structure was made of tongue-in-groove boards. The rug was bought in Egypt.

The one-room schoolhouse (BELOW) was moved to its present site between 1970 and 1972. The front door and windows were found in a reclamation yard near Palo Alto. Old wicker furniture mixed with zebra and lion skins give a late Victorian flavor to the room. A wood-burning stove heats the whole area quickly. Under the sleeping gallery, guests find a sink, stove, and stocked refrigerator, and there is always a bowl of fresh fruit on the table. The picture window is completely new; there used to be a door in its place that led to the outhouses—one for boys, one for girls.

and found salvageable Gothic Revival porches. They wall-papered and painted to hide cracks and dirt. As the house became more civilized, they turned to restoring the original adobe house and the schoolhouse.

In 1973 the roof of the main house collapsed, and the Wetzels decided to restore the whole structure. The house had to be completely taken apart, a new foundation poured, and the building painstakingly reassembled to include modern wiring and plumbing. The original redwood siding, gingerbread carving, and door and window frames were saved and stripped of seven layers of paint or duplicated with tools that Harry Wetzel made in his workshop. Several architects were consulted, but the most helpful advice came from interior designer Sandy Salmon, who helped to redesign the layout so that the rooms led naturally from one to another rather than off a central passage. New basement rooms, storage spaces, an octagonal breakfast room, and a kitchen were all added.

To make sure the kitchen would work perfectly, a prototype was constructed in plywood so that Maggie Wetzel could try out the shape and size of the cupboards and working space before they were finally built in oak and butcher block. The kitchen is full of ingenious ideas. Bottom drawers are lined with tin to make them mouse proof; an all-purpose mixer neatly folds from the working surface into a drawer below;

kitchen tools are hung around the hood of the stove on a flat brass bar that Maggie Wetzel found at a kitchen-supply shop, Dehillerain, in France.

The octagonal breakfast room is where the family congregates for casual meals or evening card games. Although it is a modern room, it has been designed with great attention to details. The octagonal arrangement of the wooden planks on the floor has been duplicated on the ceiling. An antique chandelier from Santa Rosa is made in the shape of a bunch of grapes.

Wherever possible, the original fittings have been used. For instance, the inlaid-stone corner fireplace now in the library came from another location but was original to the house.

The same care and attention have been lavished on the adobe structure near the main house. One entire wall was missing, so the Wetzels found Mr. Miller, an adobe restoration expert from Angwin, California, who made new bricks to match the old and duplicated the original woodwork. A sister building was constructed, leaving a breezeway between to be used as a carport. After the ground floor became a storeroom, there was enough space under the eaves for a self-contained apartment. The old adobe has been whitewashed inside to help preserve the adobe brick, which is far more perishable than fired brick. Since this would never have been done in Cyrus

The pedestal table (FAR LEFT) *in the dining room can seat twelve and was given to the Wetzels by a friend in Arizona. Around it, Scottish chairs with needlepoint seats are from John Bell in Aberdeen. Green moiré covers the ceiling. The faience on the table is from France. Japanese prints decorate the walls.*

In this Victorian parlor (LEFT), *Welsh, English, and American furniture mix. A gilt picture rail encircles the room. Over the mantel the two matching pictures are of Cyrus Alexander and his wife, Rufena. To the left, a smaller picture shows Captain Henry D. Fitch (1799–1849), who first commissioned Cyrus Alexander to pioneer the valley. On the oak pedestal table is a Sonoma County illustrated atlas containing a drawing made in 1877 of the Alexander house. The antique lace curtains were given by a neighbor who received them from a French family at the turn of the century. The carpet was especially made for the Turkish exhibit at the 1939 New York World's Fair.*

189

This octagonal breakfast room (LEFT) was added as an adjunct to the new kitchen. The waist-high fireplace is used for warmth and for cooking. The ancient fig tree seen through the window is more than a hundred years old, and the room was constructed so that the tree could remain in place. Wines on the table are chardonnay and pinot noir from the Alexander Valley Vineyards.

The kitchen (RIGHT) has modern features but maintains the atmosphere of an old-fashioned room. The glass in the windows is modern, but engraved in a Victorian style, and comes from a San Francisco company called Victoriana. All the cupboards and drawers in this room and the nearby passageways are oak.

Alexander's day, a small section has been left in its natural state and given a clear glass protective cover so that the original interior can be seen.

In the schoolhouse up on the hill, a scrapbook documents how the schoolhouse was taken apart, moved, and reassembled. Windows were added to give light; bathrooms replaced the boys' and girls' separate cloakrooms. A loft bedroom is reached by a staircase that has lighted treads to keep guests from stumbling in the dark. In the entrance hall is a full-length mirror made of walnut, rosewood, and inlaid fruitwood, which was made in Sonoma County in an early Victorian style.

In all three buildings, Maggie Wetzel has included some of her own personal or family treasures from her family home in Virginia. Each bedroom has a handmade quilt, all of them given to her as birthday presents from her mother, and all made by Laura Diggs of Matthews County, Virginia, who is now, alas, too old to continue her craft. Most bedrooms also include a crib for the growing number of Wetzel grandchildren. Local Alexander Valley families have donated books or pictures to the house in appreciation of the Wetzels' enthusiasm for preserving the past. The portraits of Cyrus and Rufena Alexander found on the parlor mantelpiece came from their granddaughter, Mrs. Truman Clark. "I didn't use a decorator," says Maggie Wetzel, "so it's all rather loving-hands-at-home." Nevertheless, the skill

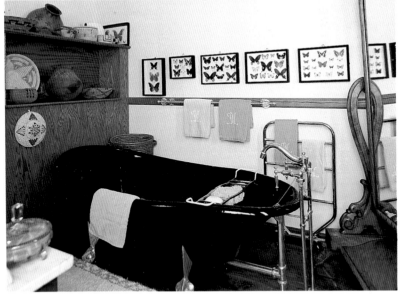

A contemporary black bathtub shares a bathroom (ABOVE) with a nineteenth-century English full-length looking glass. The shelf holds antique pots and baskets made by California Indians.

The masculine tone of the library (TOP) is set by zebra rugs, mounted African gazelle heads, and the large partners' desk that came from a Belgian bank. New oak bookcases completely cover one wall. The corner inlaid-stone fireplace was part of the original house but was moved to this room.

The front entrance leads into a small hallway (ABOVE). A zebra rug, one of Harry Wetzel's trophies, decorates the floor. The glass in the door is studded with little red stars. It came from the back door of the original house, and was moved to the front during the renovation. Inside the library, straw hats and a solar topee hang on a circa-1900 looking glass that came from Healdsburg.

she has used mixing the new with the old, and the formal with Californian ease, is impressive.

Outside, the gardens first laid out by Tom Alexander have been enlarged and improved upon by Maggie Wetzel aided by landscape designer Leland Noel of Santa Rosa. "We have chosen only to use plants one might have found during the Victorian era: peonies, delphinium, digitalis, columbine, coral bells, lavender, lilacs, iris. The iris are all divisions of the original bulbs found on the property." None of the trees have been cut, including the hundred-year-old fig tree at the back door, ancient Spanish olives, an old magnolia, an Astrakhan apple tree, and the huge oak trees. There are even redwoods that Maggie Wetzel planted by seed. Citrus trees have been planted around the newly installed swimming pool, and Bartlett pears espaliered to a wire trellis. Six varieties of table grapes are grown behind the vegetable garden, which is laid out in formal beds. A spring-fed stream that divides and flows past the house feeds the ferns, wild blackberries, and agaves, or "century plants," which thrive on its banks. Agaves are supposed to flower once a century, forming fifteen- to twenty-foot spikes that scatter millions of seeds when they die.

Within sight of the house is the newest structure, a Sonoma barn, built in a local style and intended to store hay in the loft, with space for lambing sheep and chickens below. The sheep, a flock of around sixty, are kept for their wool, some for meat, but most importantly, as a method of fire control. In the dry California summer, brush fires are a hazard, and the sheep keep the mountain grass short. Some of the chickens, a breed called Marrons, can be found in a separate coop; an English friend gave Maggie Wetzel six fertile eggs, which she brought to America and carefully incubated and hatched. These Marrons are the descendants of those six eggs.

All the Wetzel family members are involved in the vineyards and winery. Harry (Hank) Wetzel II is the wine maker and general manager; his wife, Linda, handles the bookkeeping; and their daughter, Katie, is the national sales manager. Approximately 26,000 cases of vintage-dated, varietal wines are made from 120 acres of estate-grown grapes: chardonnay, cabernet sauvignon, chenin blanc, Johannesburg riesling, gewürztraminer, pinot noir, zinfandel, and merlot. Hank Wetzel's philosophy toward making each Alexander Valley Vineyards wine is simple: handle and process the grapes as little as possible while creating a product that is pleasing to the eye, nose, palate, and budget. The winery cannot use all the grapes it grows, so only the best are selected for their wines and the rest are sold. All the grapes are handpicked in the morning while cool. Most are crushed within an hour of picking due to the short distance between the vineyard and the winery, which adds to the quality of the wine. Alexander Valley Vineyards have won, and continue to win, awards for their wines, especially their chardonnay, so the combination of hard work and family enthusiasm produces results.

In the master bedroom (LEFT), a Portuguese needlepoint carpet designed by Maggie Wetzel echoes the pink-and-green wallpaper border around the ceiling. An oval-backed carved walnut bed is a replica of the Lincoln bed in the White House. English bedside tables with oval mirrors hold lamps with Meissen porcelain figures used as bases. Behind them are tapestry fragments taken from a larger Aubusson tapestry.

Annie Alexander, wife of Tom Alexander and the last Alexander resident of the house, used this bedroom (ABOVE) until she was in her nineties. The yellow-and-white appliquéd and quilted bedcover is one of a series given to Maggie Wetzel as a young woman. The crib, originally used by Maggie Wetzel's grandmother's children, is now used for her own grandchildren.

WINERY LAKE
ARTISTRY IN A CALIFORNIA VINEYARD RESIDENCE

Off the main highway, on the byways of Napa Valley's wine country, the geometric lines of pruned grape-vines merge and separate across rolling hills. Pulling up the long drive to Winery Lake, one is confronted by an unexpected rhinoceros-fronted automobile. This is not the result of a bizarre traffic accident, but a jolting yet intriguing piece of sculpture by West Coast artist David Best. A gaggle of geese—live, not artwork—pass by haughtily. A peacock, with a great rustle of spreading wings, flaunts his feathers like a Folies Bergères showgirl. "Here come the invaders!" is René di Rosa's greeting. He is not your average farmer, nor is his dwelling a typical farmhouse. Yet he has been a successful farmer for the last quarter of a century and has been able to mix the labor of grape growing with the pleasure of collecting art.

René di Rosa and his wife, Veronica, live in a house that was originally built with no intention of it ever being a dwelling. More than one hundred years ago, two Frenchmen, Michel Debret and Pierre Priet, bought some farming land in the Carneros region of the southern Napa Valley, which they planted as vineyards. To convert their grapes into wine, they built a winery, which is the structure that the di Rosas now occupy.

The land that the Frenchmen bought had been used previously for general farming, and earlier farmers had cleared the

Originally a crude stone winery built over a century ago, this building (LEFT) is now a fascinating home and art gallery.

A peacock (RIGHT) poses for the camera. This is one of twenty-six that live at Winery Lake.

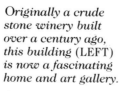

Connecting buildings off the graveled courtyard (LEFT) include a barn, Veronica di Rosa's studio— the dormer window lights the self-contained apartment above it— shelter for tractors (and peacocks), and an apartment for Mr. di Rosa's mother. At the far left is a piece of sculpture that dominates the center of the courtyard, Rainbowing Prism, *by California artist Charles Ross.*

Lines of winter-pruned grapevines (ABOVE) form op art patterns across the slopes of Winery Lake's vineyards.

land of all the large surface rocks so that the fields could be plowed and planted. These rocks were then used by the farmers to make stone fences that marked the boundaries of their fields and kept their animals from straying.

Michel and Pierre used these fieldstones to build their winery, taking them from a wall on a hill above the site because the heavy rocks were easier to transport downward. It is thought that Mexican laborers helped to build the structure, which was cleverly planned to nestle into a hillside slope. This gave the building one entrance on the higher level to bring the grapes in, and another exit at the lower level to take the wine out. No windows were necessary, so none were made. Nor were there any partitions in the building; the interior plan was simply one big room upstairs and another big room below. Evidently operating on an austere budget, the Frenchmen could not afford to chink the winery with concrete, so a mixture of sand and lime was used as mortar.

When the winery was operating, the grapes were crushed on the top floor and the juice flowed by gravity to the barrels on the floor below where the wine aged in the cool cellar-like room that had been dug into the hillside. This was the traditional method used for making wine, and although many Californian enologists have experimented with other methods, such as pumping the juice, most have returned to this slower but surer procedure.

197

Separating the hall from the living area are old doors with panels that can be opened and closed like Dutch doors (LEFT). Wine bottles decorating the door lights on either side of the entrance were made by a craftsman from Santa Barbara (or, as René di Rosa likes to say, "a Santa Barbarian").

Wine is stored in this room and in the corner room behind the curved archway (ABOVE LEFT). To accommodate wine tasting, this room also has a sink, a dishwasher, and cupboards of glasses. Around the walls are grape baskets, bottle stands, and huge baskets of corks.

A headless, transparent man sculpted by Manual Neri sits in front of the French doors (ABOVE RIGHT). Next to him is a piece called Half Red Books *by Jim Pomeroy.*

The Carneros region was ideal for grape growing, but the wine industry was to suffer two body blows that all but finished it as a commercial venture for the first half of the twentieth century. A root disease called phylloxera, caused by plant lice, killed the vines and spread all over the area, forcing many vineyards to go out of business. Those that hung on were then hit by Prohibition, when wine making became illegal.

For a few years during the thirties the winery operated as an illicit still, producing inferior hooch, until the Internal Revenue caught up with the operation and closed it down. For a short time after that, the cellar of the winery was used to raise mushrooms, but finally it became a mere storage place until René di Rosa found it. "I wasn't buying the building," he says. "I was buying the land to plant as vineyards."

Mr. di Rosa traces his interest in wine back to his childhood when his Italian father would put a teaspoon of wine into his glass of water. Plain water was made much more interesting when it was colored with red wine. His father, who was the Italian consul general in New York, made wine in their cellar with his Italian gardener. Wine was part of the family's diet.

René di Rosa moved to the West Coast and became a reporter for the *San Francisco Chronicle*. He lived an urban existence until, at age forty, he got the urge to take up a country pursuit. In 1960 he scouted the area north of San Francisco and discovered the Carneros region, which at the time was generally bleak and uncultivated. He remembered an old Italian saying: "If you can't grow anything else on a piece of land, plant an olive or a grapevine." He found an olive grove and, nearby, Pierre and Michel's winery, a reminder that there had once been grapes in the region. The idea of bringing back the past appealed to him, although, at that point, more from a romantic than a practical point of view. He started to study books on

The cellar of the old winery was where the grape juice was collected, made into wine, and bottled. Here is a collection of old wine-making paraphernalia, including grape baskets, bottle baskets, wine kegs, bungs, bottles, and funnels. Pinned to an upright support are slogans Mr. di Rosa invented to promote the vineyard.

When the century-old winery was converted into a dwelling, a fieldstone tower with a witch's hat turret was added as a second entrance. This makes an ideal mud room (RIGHT). The rope tolls a bell lodged in the top of the tower.

This living area, photographed from the second-floor gallery, is used for working, dining, and entertaining and provides a background for a collection of works by talented artists from the San Francisco Bay area. Over the fireplace is a painting by Robert Arneson entitled The Big Grape of Winery Lake. (Mr. di Rosa is holding the grape.) Other artists represented in this collection include John Buck, Roy De Forrest, Robert Hudson, and Richard Shaw.

This fireplace (ABOVE) was designed to display the two carved stone male figures that support the mantel. The gargantuan ceramic jar is by David Best. On the far side of the fireplace, the rabbit sculpture is by Karen Breschi. A comfortable seat in the foreground is made of ceramic, with a handwoven seat pad.

viticulture, which he obtained from the University of California at Davis. Gradually he started to plant his vineyards. He admits that much of his success was due to his timing. "I did it at the right time. Louis Martini was the only other person with a vineyard here. There simply were not enough grapes for the growing wine industry."

René di Rosa proved to be a masterly vineyardist. His first grapes were planted by off-duty sailors from a nearby naval base. They were men who had been brought up on farms, liked to drive tractors, and were not afraid of a hard day's work. Some of them return every now and then to see what has happened to the vineyard since.

No longer the biggest vineyard in Carneros, Winery Lake is the best known in the area for the high quality of its grapes. Over a period of eight years, 200 acres were planted with five varieties: pinot noir and merlot for the reds, and chardonnay, Johannesburg riesling, and gewürztraminer for the whites. Today the vineyard supplies grapes to more than a dozen wineries, and, in some cases, the Winery Lake appellation, denoting the source of the grapes, is printed in larger lettering than the name of the wine maker.

While work was going on in the vineyard, Mr. di Rosa was transforming the winery into a home. This was a formidable task that had to be achieved gradually as the grape business brought in the money. A large part of the renovation was to

This sitting room is part of Veronica di Rosa's self-contained apartment over her studio. The dormer window was built with an arched top to echo some of the windows and French doors in the main house. The stained and polished floors and off-white walls were installed about ten years ago. The maple rocking chair is North American, circa 1850. A Chinese export tobacco jar is displayed on the windowsill.

The di Rosas' bedroom (LEFT) is photographed through a mirror to show the peacock posing on the balustrade outside. Books, erotic drawings, and assorted artworks lure the eye. The antique gold-embroidered velvet coverlet on the back of the settee was a gift from French guests.

The guest room bed (ABOVE) provides a perfect setting for this sculpture by Manual Neri. The figure lies on a witty patchwork quilt that Veronica di Rosa made from her husband's workshirts, including in the patch pockets, buttons, and tabs. She also made the curtains, which are tied back with braid and cowbells. On the window ledge is a delicately carved and painted wooden snake that metamorphoses into a pair of legs and is set in a box, created by Michael Stevens. Telescope sculpture on the chest of drawers is an early Tom Holland. Gene Beery's It's Only A Painting *hangs on the wall.*

make the building safe, even though it had stood firm for a century. Mr. di Rosa was concerned because the area is prone to earthquakes and he did not want to fix up the house only to see it later reduced to rubble. The original lime and sand chinking was replaced with concrete. In addition, the structure was given steel supports, "not as architectural trivia," the owner points out, "but as essential construction."

He planned to make the large room at the top of the structure into living quarters, and the cool, dark bottom room into offices and a wine cellar. As the design evolved, windows had to be opened up and framed. The living quarters had to include one room big enough to display a growing art collection, which had many pieces on a huge scale. In addition, Mr. di Rosa had amassed other artifacts over the years, such as an antique wrought-iron Spanish pulpit and two carved stone male cary-

atids, bought at auction from the Hearst collections, and he had to find places to incorporate them in his new house. The caryatids now frame a fireplace in the living area; the pulpit hangs in a turreted tower built near the kitchen entrance.

Although the main living area is an immense floor-to-ceiling room, a second floor was added across part of the space to provide a smaller upper room that can also be used to display works of art. A narrow gallery leading from it runs across one entire length of the room. This is where the balustrades from the University of California's School of Mining found a home. Beneath this, the second floor was partitioned into smaller rooms: a master bedroom, a bathroom with a huge green-marble sunken tub, two dressing rooms, a corridor of closets, a guest room, and a bathroom adjoining it, which can also be entered from the vestibule off the main entrance.

The bathroom has a lush tropical
atmosphere. The mural by Marilyn
Rabinowich blends with the green
marble of the lower walls and the
sunken tub with two showers. On
the far wall holding a faucet is a
sculpture by James Melchert
modeled on his wife's hand.

The second entrance, beneath the turreted tower, forms a
circular mud room, essential because the twenty-four peacocks
that roam the courtyard outside are messy creatures. Muddy
boots, damp raincoats, vegetables to be cleaned, and flowers to
be trimmed can all be left in this room, which has been tiled
in a rustic fashion and leads into the large, sunny, and practical kitchen.

An iron spiral staircase in the living area leads both up to
the gallery and down into the cellar. This nineteenth-century
staircase came from the Alcazar Theater in San Francisco,
where stars such as W. C. Fields and Mae West used to perform
before it was torn down.

The large room on the ground floor has been partitioned
into three small offices, one large room used to display wine-
making paraphernalia, works of art, and Mr. di Rosa's collection of antique wagons, and a wine-tasting room equipped
with a modern sink unit and refrigerator and cupboards full
of glasses. In addition, there is an inner room where wine
is stored.

Every room in the house shows evidence of a passion for
modern art, particularly the work of artists from the San Francisco Bay area. These are witty, intriguing, impudent, sensual
pieces that have been cunningly placed to hold the eye and
provoke attention. Even looking out the windows becomes an
adventure because the peacocks pose on the outdoor railings
and frequently scream at each other.

Veronica di Rosa, a watercolorist and illustrator, works in
a studio in the carriage house across the graveled courtyard.
Above the studio is a newly built apartment where she can escape from the bustle of vineyard business. The furnishings here
are calm and pleasant, a mixture of modern comfort with easy-
to-like antiques, stacks of vintage illustrated children's books,
bowls of fruit and flowers. This is where Veronica di Rosa's
children, now grown up, can stay when they come to visit.

Increasingly, the di Rosas are turning to art collecting as
their main occupation, and to this end they have sold their 250
acres of well-established vineyard to Seagrams. The di Rosas
are now involved with the further challenge of creating an art
park on their remaining 230 acres, where emerging artists can
show their work. The lake, which was formed from a small
pond, and the winery house are to become part of this complex. They are committed to creating an environment where
art can blossom and be enjoyed. Their home is such a place
and a unique American farmhouse.

207

PIEDRA BLANCA RANCHO
A VICTORIAN FAMILY CATTLE RANCH
IN SAN SIMEON, CALIFORNIA

The main ranch house (LEFT) was constructed in 1863 for George and Phoebe Hearst and also to provide a residence for a ranch manager when the Hearsts were living in San Francisco. Surrounded by formal gardens and fenced off from the rest of the ranch compound, this mid-Victorian house is softened by the Gothic Revival detailing on the porch and roof brackets.

The office building (RIGHT) is adorned with elk antlers found on the ranch. Horseshoes decorate the porch supports, which were designed to hold the reins of horses.

Along California's Highway 1, with the Pacific on one side and brush-scattered grazing land rising to mountains on the other, an almost surrealistic vision of a herd of zebras might appear. Perfectly content, the animals chew grass alongside Hereford cattle, oblivious to the cars speeding by. Is this an American version of the Serengeti Plain? The sequence becomes even dreamier as a fairytale castle appears, perched on top of the mountains.

This is San Simeon, a tiny town whose main industry is catering to the tourists who flock to the famous Hearst Castle, which is open every day of the year but Christmas and Thanksgiving. Less obviously marked but nearby is the entrance to the Piedra Blanca Rancho, which, though part of the Hearst estate, is a private ranch.

Work, for the ranch hands, starts early. At seven in the morning, a truck horn honks and a dozen or so quarter horses gallop over the rugged grass and brush-covered terrain to gather for the morning roundup. Silently but never stopping or wasting a gesture, the cowboys brush down their mounts, then lay colorful Navaho-style blankets across their horses' backs and, on top of them, ample western saddles. Then the horses are herded into trucks that drive them to the section of this large ranch where they will be working for the day. The cow-

The Bunkhouse (LEFT), designed by Julia Morgan, the architect of the Hearst Castle, was built in the 1920s to house as many as fifty ranch hands. Single, double, and triple bedrooms lead off from the open corridor. A passage with a tiled roof leads to one of two communal and somewhat spartan bathrooms.

Modern wrought-iron gates (ABOVE) leading to the Piedra Blanca Rancho depict decorative wagon wheels. Cattle on the sign show it to be a grazing ranch. On the far distant mountains is the Hearst Castle.

boys' dogs—border collies and Australian shepherds—sit expectantly in the cab of the truck. The trucks carry cowboys, dogs, and horses off to corral the calves for branding.

The ranch has belonged to the Hearst family since the middle of the nineteenth century when George Hearst purchased a Spanish land grant of 50,000 acres, which is still intact today. Before the Hearsts husbanded the land, the conquistadors used an overland route from Mexico to San Francisco—the Portola Trail—which runs right through part of the ranch.

The Salinan Indians inhabited this area before the Mexicans and the Spaniards. They were nomads who ranged throughout the highest coastline in the world—the Santa Lucia Mountains—which were named by Sebastián Vizcaíno, the navigator who sailed past these jagged outcroppings on Saint Lucia's day in 1602. It is believed that the city of Salinas, to the northeast of the ranch, is named after this tribe. Little else is known of them because, like many Indian tribes, they were either expelled from their ancestral lands or succumbed to the Europeans' diseases. Their only legacy is a few hollowed-out stone mortars used for grinding grain, which can be seen in the Hearst Castle.

During the first half of the nineteenth century, San Simeon was a whaling port. Relics of those days—huge pots that were used to boil down blubber into lamp oil—can be found by the shore of the tiny seacoast village. During George Hearst's time, San Simeon became a dairy-farming area whose cheese was sold as far north as San Francisco. Products had to be sent up the coast by boat, because the high winding roads, which can still be treacherous today, had not yet been developed for regular transport.

The ranch land was used then, as now, for grazing, but farming was only one of George Hearst's activities. He had come west from Missouri and become successful in the mining business. By an interesting coincidence, he formed a triumvirate partnership with William Tevis and Ben Ali Haggin, who at one time owned what is now Normandy Farm in Kentucky (see page 92). The trio—Hearst, Haggin, and Tevis—became well known in California for their various enterprises and investments. Tevis established the Wells Fargo Stage Company.

Tucked under the stairs is a 1920s gramophone that has been electrified. The low pedestal table holds a collection of hats worn by William Randolph Hearst when he was on the ranch.

Heavy late Victorian dining room chairs are softened for twentieth-century comfort with seat cushions (LEFT). Early nineteenth-century Chinese export vases, jugs, and tobacco jars decorate the mantel, and more pieces are displayed inside the corner vitrines.

Rococo Revival chairs of carved rosewood (BELOW) surround a card table whose silk top has been worn to "a pleasing decay." The American mirror, side table, crystal lamps, and glass vase all came from the Phoebe Hearst house in Pleasanton, near San Francisco.

Haggin formed the Kern County Land Company and was responsible for the founding of the Santa Anita racetrack. George Hearst, also a horseman, was one of the charter members of the Jockey Club, the organization that governs American horse-racing activities. He developed the Anaconda Mining Company in Montana, founded the Homestate Mining Company in South Dakota, had numerous mining interests in Mexico, and eventually became a senator.

Once he had established himself in California, Hearst went back to Missouri to claim the woman he loved, schoolteacher Phoebe Apperson. In 1863 he built the main house on Piedra Blanca as their residence on the ranch. A large, two-storied wooden structure surmounted by a square cupola, the house was built during the period when several different styles of architecture were fashionable, all of them romantic rather than classical in tone. Often generally termed Victorian, these houses were sometimes inspired by the Gothic Revival or the Italianate style. The Piedra Blanca ranch house, like many others in California for the well-to-do, is a mixture of both. The basic structure—sometimes called a cube and cupola house—has a simple hipped roof in the Italianate mode, but the roof brackets and carving on the porch are Gothic Revival. Breakthroughs in technology—the perfection of the scroll saw and the lathe—made elaborate wood carving possible, although the decoration on this house is restrained compared to many houses of the period. Neither the name of the architect nor the builder is on record.

Making good use of her husband's affluence, Phoebe Apperson Hearst turned her attention to philanthropy, women's causes in particular. She met an American student architect, Julia Morgan, in Paris and offered to finance the young woman's education at the Ecole des Beaux-Arts—making her the first foreign female to attend the school—but her offer was declined. Admiring the independent Miss Morgan, Phoebe Hearst asked her to design many of the buildings she donated to the University of California. Julia Morgan helped to design the Hearst Memorial Mining Building, which was erected in memory of George Hearst. The metal balustrades from the School of Mining now decorate the gallery at Winery Lake, another California house (seen page 205).

Historical restoration fired Phoebe Hearst's interest. She

and her only son, William Randolph, helped to restore most of the original Spanish missions in California. She was also responsible for the initial restoration of George Washington's estate at Mount Vernon. She sponsored archaeological digs in Egypt and other parts of the world, helping to recover treasures that would otherwise have been lost to the encroachments of modern life. And, not abandoning her teaching profession, she became one of the founders of the Parent-Teacher Association, or PTA.

Her son, William Randolph Hearst, was evidently equally impressed by the work of Julia Morgan. He financed an 8,000-seat theater for the University of California, which Morgan designed to resemble the Greek theater at Epidaurus. A photograph of William Randolph Hearst giving a speech at the opening ceremony now hangs in the butler's pantry at Piedra Blanca Rancho. He went on to use her for what he first discussed with her as "a few Jappo-Swisso" bungalows on the hills of his ranch at San Simeon. In 1919 he started off thinking that what he wanted were simple, rustic structures, but by 1942 and $4.7 million later, the flamboyant Hearst Castle was the result. Designed by Morgan after endless changes, the twin-towered castle now dominates the crest of the mountain, while three elaborate guest houses sweep down the hillside; a Greco-Roman temple is reflected in the "Neptune" swimming pool, and the whole gigantic and preposterous complex is surrounded by groves of trees and herds of wild animals roaming the landscape.

Phoebe Apperson Hearst must have transmitted her passion for old artifacts to her son, for he was to turn the acquisition of antiques into a mania. He scoured the world for possessions, many of dubious aesthetic value, to incorporate or display in his castle. He never stopped accumulating, and when he died in 1951, there were still cases of uncrated antiques on the New York docks whose contents were eventually auctioned at Gimbel's.

William Randolph Hearst added to the Piedra Blanca Rancho in several other ways. He added another 165,000 acres to the original 50,000-acre grant, which then required more ranch hands to run it. To accommodate the cowboys he built the Bunkhouse, commissioning Julia Morgan to design something suitable. This time she was allowed to come up with a simple structure based on what is often called the Monterey style, which is a free revival of the Anglo-influenced Spanish colonial houses of northern California. The stuccoed building has a roof of curved Spanish tiles and a long porch corridor with doors leading off to various different-sized bedrooms that can sleep, in total, fifty people. Two large single-story communal bathrooms lead off the corridor to the back of the building, while a kitchen and communal dining room terminate one end of the structure; and a large lounge, or "bull room" as it is called, completes the other. The mood of the Bunkhouse, in spite of the traditional Spanish-inspired stucco and tile, is en-

A large kitchen (LEFT) at one end of the Bunkhouse can produce banquets if necessary. The stove, manufactured in Los Angeles by Madsen Ironworks, is mainly a conversation piece, although it was used up until the 1960s. Next to this kitchen is a dining room that can feed whole conventions of the Hearst companies.

Framed family photographs line the walls of the butler's pantry (ABOVE).

The furnishings for this master bedroom came from the Phoebe Hearst house in Pleasanton. The portrait of her between the windows was painted by Orrin Peck, who was one of her protégés. The maple head- and footboards on the beds are painted with scenes of nymphs and cupids. The rosewood chairs are in the Rococo Revival style of the mid-nineteenth century.

tirely twentieth century and contrasts pleasingly with the main ranch house. Because most of the present-day ranch hands live in separate houses away from the main ranch house and its satellite buildings, the Bunkhouse is now used as a spillover for guests, for Hearst Corporation conferences, and for family celebrations.

At the beginning of World War II, Hearst sold the 165,000 acreage to the United States Army as training grounds, on condition that they sell it back to him if they had no more use for it. So far, the army has always found reasons to keep it.

Although Piedra Blanca is owned by the Hearst estate, Jack and Phoebe Cooke (she is William Randolph Hearst's granddaughter) are the official residents of the ranch house. Jack Cooke manages the agricultural concerns of the Hearst estate. The ranch uses between forty and fifty quarter horses to

herd about 4,000 head of beef cattle, mostly Herefords. A curious weather pattern makes the area unsuitable for wheat growing; in late July and through August, heavy clouds will not let the sun through to ripen a grain harvest. Although some vegetable crops might thrive under these conditions, the ranch is too remote to ship such crops with ease.

The Piedra Blanca ranch house stands today much as it did when it was first built. Set apart from the other ranch buildings—an office, barns, the Bunkhouse, and a smaller residence for the ranch manager—the house is surrounded by formal flower gardens, flowering shrubs, gravel walks, and a wooden fence. There have been no major structural changes outside, and even inside, the changes have been gradual.

When the house was built in 1863, no doubt George and Phoebe Hearst were able to afford and indeed insisted on all the

A *charmingly old-fashioned upstairs bathroom* (LEFT) *has a marble-topped washbasin. At the far end, a child's commode has a tray to hold playthings.*

A *guest room* (ABOVE) *is decorated in a red-striped paisley pattern chosen by Mrs. Cooke. The mattress on the bed is made of real horsehair—"the creeping mattress," says the housekeeper, Mrs. Ortega, who finds the coverlet wrinkles each time it is smoothed out. Here, as in each bedroom, is a washbasin set on a corner cupboard. By the fireplace is a copper warming pan once used to heat the bed.*

latest amenities. Indoor plumbing was in its infancy, but every bedroom was equipped with its own built-in washbasin set into a wooden cupboard, which was often tucked into a corner. The porcelain basins were coordinated with the colors of the room. One has a charming willow-patterned bowl; another is decorated with pale pink bands of color. They must have seemed very modern and luxurious at the time they were installed. The fireplaces still have their original painted tiles, but they have been converted to gas to ease the housekeeping chores. The kitchen area has probably seen the most changes. There were cooking ranges by the 1860s, which would have been wood burning; the sink would have been made of stone, and there would have been an icebox instead of a refrigerator. The central ceiling fixtures would have held kerosene lamps, later possibly gas-lit lamps, but by the end of the nineteenth century, electricity was beginning to be used and the Hearsts would have welcomed the convenience.

Jack and Phoebe Cooke have maintained the ranch house in its original style wherever possible without sacrificing any of its comfort. Mrs. Cooke has selected all the drapery and upholstery fabrics with the help of Austine Hearst, her aunt. They have chosen carpets and bed covers that preserve the Victorian feeling of the house. Much of the furniture, the ornaments, and the pictures have been brought from Phoebe Apperson Hearst's house in Pleasanton, a town in the East Bay area of San Francisco, where she maintained a residence when away from the ranch. The demeanor of the house indicates high-minded respectability, the most prized quality of the Victorian matron. Phoebe Hearst Cooke's great-grandmother and namesake would be well pleased by Piedra Blanca today.

RANCHO SANTA CLARA DEL NORTE

CALIFORNIA CITRUS FARMING IN VENTURA COUNTY

Built by Juan Sanchez in the 1830s, the original house (LEFT) was a one-story adobe building. A second story made of wood was added in 1900 by Leopoldo and Amparo Schiappa Pietra, along with the fountain and flowerbeds.

Simple turned-wood columns are topped with Ionic capitals. Some of them are set on painted adobe brick foundations (RIGHT). These columns support the porch that surrounds the whole house and was part of the turn-of-the-century renovation. The fruit came from trees on the ranch.

D awn breaks over the distant mountains north of Los Angeles, making the irrigated fields glisten in the early sun. Crop workers head out for their day's labor amid some of the finest citrus- and vegetable-growing country in the world.

This idyllic part of America, with its balmy climate, was richly endowed by nature even when it was inhabited solely by the peace-loving Chumash Indians. Chumash women were regarded for their skill at basketry and the men for fishing. Their canoes were painted red and decorated with shells. Their pueblos of spherically shaped huts along the beaches were observed by the first European explorers just fifty years after Columbus discovered America. The Portuguese navigator Juan Rodriguez Cabrillo, sailing under the flag of Spain, voyaged up the California coast with two caravels and came to what is now called Ventura. He stayed for two weeks with the Chumash.

Spanish occupation of California became official in 1769. Gaspar de Portola became California's first governor. On an overland expedition to Monterey, he reached the Santa Clara River on August 13, 1769, and diarists in his entourage also were impressed by the Chumash Indians' skill at constructing and handling their canoes. Father Crespi, the priest, envisioned "a mission on this good site to which nothing is lack-

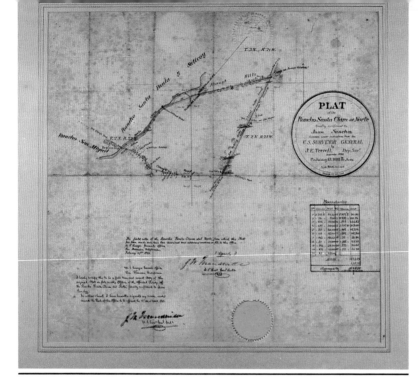

An early map shows the acreage of the Rancho Santa Clara del Norte when it was first granted to Juan Sanchez.

ing," and indeed, a mission, San Buenaventura, was founded in 1782. A 1917 pamphlet, *History of Santa Barbara, San Luis Obispo and Ventura Counties,* reports: "On that day, Easter, it was founded in solemn ceremonies. . . . in the presence of the assembled Indians, whose emotions we cannot know, a cross was raised and a mass was sung and a sermon was preached." The mission became the dominating feature of the region and, being on El Camino Real, lay in the pathway of traveling priests, officials, ranchers, merchants, traders, and settlers. Eventually the name of the mission, San Buenaventura, became shortened, and the city that grew around it was called Ventura.

Due to Mexico's successful revolt against Spain in 1822, California became Mexican territory. The mission declined gradually and each year trained fewer neophytes and commanded less power and owned fewer cattle. The Indians wandered away, many to work on the growing number of ranches. In 1836 the mission was secularized, and by 1839 there were only 300 Chumash left. The presence of the white people had broken their spirit and had produced a deep inward depression. They had been decimated by the white men's diseases and shunted off their own lands. Today the Chumash are gone.

Around the middle of the nineteenth century, the first one-story adobe house of the Rancho Santa Clara del Norte was built by Juan Sanchez. He had been granted the original 13,988 acres of the ranch in about 1830. It is believed that Sanchez fell deeply into debt and sold his land to two enterprising Italian brothers, Federico and Antonio Schiappa Pietra, who had

220

Behind the house is a small family chapel that was consecrated in 1928 and is still in use.

A *wide variety of camellias blossom under the arbor in Rancho Santa Clara del Norte's garden* (LEFT).

made their money by operating general stores in Santa Barbara and Ventura. They purchased the land for sixty cents an acre in 1862. Another brother, Leopoldo, joined them when on leave from his ministry of public works for the Italian government in 1866. He had intended to return to Italy, but when Federico died in 1867, Leopoldo stayed on to manage and improve the ranch, which had been started as a sheep and cattle business. In 1890 the two surviving brothers changed from the stock business to general farming, raising principally barley and corn at first and finally concentrating on lima beans, planting 7,000 acres that were watered by an irrigation ditch from the nearby Santa Clara River. During a very dry season in 1891, they gave permission to squatters to work in the opening of this canal. Leopoldo owned a controlling interest because he was the vice president of the Santa Clara Water and Irrigating Company.

Antonio and Leopoldo Schiappa Pietra returned to Italy in 1894 on a semi-permanent basis, and shortly after, Antonio died in San Remo. Leopoldo thus became the sole heir to the large and valuable interests in California, and he returned to live in Los Angeles, where he built an elaborate house in a Moorish architectural style. Later, on a visit to Italy, he was made a cavalier of the crown of Italy by King Umberto.

Leopoldo Schiappa Pietra married Amparo Arenas, who was a member of one of the oldest and most distinguished families in California. Her mother was Doña Josefa Palomares de Arenas. When Josefa was born, the pueblo, or town, of Los Angeles was only thirty-four years old. There were no schools at the time but she was so anxious to learn that she saved every scrap of wrapping paper with writing on it that came from Spain. She received a primary reader, but few other books were available. At age fourteen she married Don José Maria

The handsome staircase flanked by Ionic pillars (FAR LEFT) was part of the turn-of-the-century renovation. An early nineteenth-century American grandfather clock on the left belonged to Mr. Lloyd-Butler's father's family and came from New Brunswick.

Tiny boxes (LEFT) have been collected over the years by the Lloyd-Butlers for their daughter, Camilla. In the black velvet frame is a picture of Cynthia Lloyd-Butler's maternal grandmother, Herminia Julia Ortiz Oreña. The small Madonna was made in Mexico about 1930–1940 by Diego Cortes; the large Virgin in a blue cloak is Nuestra Señora de los Remedios.

From the upstairs landing, the family chapel is visible through the tympanum of the Palladian-style window (ABOVE). In the center of the windowsill sits a small 1850 chest. On either side are Sheffield champagne coolers bought in the 1930s. To the right is a Gothic carved-wood triptych depicting St. Anthony. To the left is a pair of Staffordshire dogs.

223

This circa-1840 silver repoussé dresser set was collected, piece by piece, by Cynthia Lloyd-Butler's mother after she was given a brush marked with her grandmother's initials: M.A.L. for Maria Antonia Lataillard. She was the daughter of the last commandant of the presidio in Santa Barbara.

In the master bedroom a Venetian-glass mirror (RIGHT) belonged to Mrs. Lloyd-Butler's great-aunt, Julia Ortiz Weiler. A collection of brushes, buttonhooks, letter openers, and nail files has been put together from larger, broken-up silver dresser sets that belonged to the Lloyd-Butler and Oreña families.

The dining room (FAR LEFT) was enlarged at the end of the nineteenth century from two smaller rooms. The lace and linen Madeira tablecloth belonged to Julia Ortiz Weiler, a sister of Cynthia Lloyd-Butler's grandmother. The pattern on the Bavarian plates is called Santa Rosa; the camellias are from the camellia arbor in the garden.

The living room (LEFT) was made into its present size in 1939 when a center adobe wall was removed. Previously there were two rooms, a formal parlor and the ranch office. Paintings over the yellow sofa include an 1874 Daubigny landscape and an 1862 J. T. Herring farm scene. In the far corner is a 1932 Diego Rivera, and above the velvet-covered sofa is a seventeenth-century painting by David Teniers.

A guest wing above the kitchen area was originally built for servants (BELOW).

Avila, whose ancestors were Mexican and whose family owned large tracts of land in the Los Angeles area. After his death she remarried and from this second marriage, to Luis Arenas, produced one son, Frank, who became governor of Baja California in 1868, and three daughters, Aurelia, Amparo, and Luisa. The eldest, Aurelia, married Charles Ross, a Scotsman, and they produced two sons and two daughters before the marriage ended in divorce. Aurelia died in 1900 when her children were still young, and so they were reared and educated by her sister, Amparo, who had married Leopoldo Schiappa Pietra.

The Ross children were the principal heirs of Leopoldo's estate. Ida Ross, the third child, inherited the "home ranch" portion of the Rancho Santa Clara del Norte. Unlike her grandmother, Doña Josefa, Ida had all the benefits of a fine education and she led a cosmopolitan life, traveling extensively in Europe. In 1915 she married John Lloyd-Butler at St. Patrick's Cathedral in New York. He was the son of Samuel Melvin Butler, president of the Asphaltum and Oil Refining Company of Los Angeles, and Julia Lloyd, the daughter of a shipowner in St. John's, New Brunswick.

Upon marrying Ida, John Lloyd-Butler took up an agricultural career and managed his wife's property. For several decades he was the president of the Santa Clara Water and Irrigating Company, just as Ida's uncle had been, served as president of the Ventura County Fair in 1925, and was a member of the board of directors of several agricultural co-ops.

227

A guest room (LEFT) with twin beds has an 1865 walnut dressing table that was part of a collection of furniture belonging to Cynthia Lloyd-Butler's mother. In the corner the desk with finials is also walnut and was used by her maternal grandmother. The tole tray used as a small table was a gift from James Lloyd-Butler to his wife. The toy train is part of their son's collection.

Guests sleep in a Federal-style post bed in this sunny bedroom (RIGHT). The small American Victorian loveseat belonged to Cynthia Lloyd-Butler's grandmother, Herminia Oreña, and came from her house in Los Angeles. On it are cushions needlepointed by Mrs. Lloyd-Butler.

He and Ida had five children: Sheila, Shane, Clare, Patrick, and James. The youngest, James, now lives with his wife, Cynthia, in the house that the Schiappa Pietra brothers purchased from Juan Sanchez. The ranch belongs to the surviving heirs of John Lloyd-Butler: Shane, Patrick, and James and their children. James Lloyd-Butler operates the family property.

In 1900 Leopoldo and Amparo made extensive additions to the original adobe brick house. The Far West had plentiful supplies of softwood, which could be machine cut into standard lengths, thicknesses, and widths of lumber. Nails had become cheap and plentiful, and these technological advances made possible new framing systems for houses. The platform, or western frame, was one. This method allows each story of the building to be erected as a separate unit—indeed, each wall is built as a separate entity—and hoisted into place. This enables work to progress simultaneously on different units and speeds up the building process. It was a perfect method for erecting the second, wood-framed story of the Schiappa Pietra house.

The new floor was added in the newly popular Neoclassical style with a strong California flavor in the mixture of the classical front pediment and the adobe-based porch pillars.

Inside, an impressive staircase was constructed that divided at the intermediate landing just below a Palladian-style window facing the back of the house. The large dining room to the right of the front door was created from two smaller rooms and a kitchen wing was added to the back of the house with servants' quarters above. The porch with wood Ionic columns was wrapped around all sides of the house. All the mill work was done in the nearby town of Saticoy.

The gardens were laid out at this time in the fashionable turn-of-the-century style with formal beds, clipped hedges, fountain, camellia arbor, and, of course, palm trees—which are not native to the area but were added as a status symbol to the balmy Californian garden.

A family chapel, added in the 1920s and consecrated in 1928, is directly behind the main house and centered on an axis with the Palladian window. Several barns and a gardener-

The baroque gilt looking glass (ABOVE), which is Italian, has been in the house since the days of Leopoldo Schiappa Pietra. The antique Hepplewhite chest below it also belonged to the Schiappa Pietra family. On it is a collection of tortoiseshell brushes, combs, and mirrors that came from Cynthia Lloyd-Butler's family. The portrait in the flower-sprigged frame is of one of her grandmother's nieces.

Avocados are one of the many crops that flourish in this area (RIGHT). They are reached by long aluminum ladders balanced by a single pole for support, which can be placed deep into the hard, shiny foliage of the avocado trees.

The tiny garden shed (BELOW) has a roof of handmade tiles from the original adobe house, which accounts for their outsize scale.

caretaker's house are all part of the current complex. Surrounding the buildings and gardens are lemon, orange, and avocado trees, which are now the main crops of the ranch. James Lloyd-Butler can remember that when he was a boy, walnuts and lima beans were the main product. At the present time, some of the land is rented out to tenant farmers who grow whatever they feel the market needs, such as celery, lettuce, or other vegetables and instant turf.

James and Cynthia Lloyd-Butler lived for many years in the neighboring town of Oxnard, and much of the furniture in the ranch house came from there. Other pieces came from James Lloyd-Butler's family—either from Riverside, California, where his father lived, or from St. John's, New Brunswick, where his mother was born—as well as from his wife's ancestors. Some of the furniture is reproduction, chosen to fit the scale of the house, but is softened by the pleasant accumulation of family mementos, like the silver-framed photographs that cluster on the piano and the antique tortoiseshell brushes collected on a dressing table. A strong Spanish influence is felt throughout the house in the form of carved wooden Madonnas, paintings of convivial cardinals, and the occasional cross or saintly triptych. The impression is not one of oppressive religiosity but a statement of lineage, belief, and family stability that has allowed and encouraged such an assemblage.

The house, by size and layout, is made for gatherings, not just of objects but of people. One envisions large, lively families, sit-down dinners for twelve or twenty, dances in the entrance hall, wedding parties on the lawn. When Cynthia Lloyd-Butler entertains, she likes to use the old silver and china. The house has been used for wine tastings, and there have been many parties and afternoon teas for philanthropic organizations. Due in no small measure to the present management and trustees, the Rancho Santa Clara del Norte is as warm and welcoming in its distinctively Californian way as the coziest classic stone farmhouse in Pennsylvania.

230

In the heart of the finest citrus-growing country in the world, the ranch hands harvest lemons (LEFT).

This horse barn (ABOVE) was converted into a walnut dehydrator by John Lloyd-Butler in the 1920s, when walnuts were a principal crop of the ranch. Now it is used mainly for storage.

Because of the changing nature of commerce, no source list can ever be complete despite every effort at accuracy. Here, therefore, is a somewhat quirky, gleaned-along-the-way listing of goods, services, and publications that may be of use to readers. An asterisk (*) appears next to those listings that deal only through architects or decorators.

ANTIQUES, COUNTRY ACCESSORIES

AMERICA HURRAH ANTIQUES
766 Madison Avenue
New York, NY 10021
(212) 535-1930
Great collection of antique American quilts; American folk art and antiques including country furniture, decoys, Indian artifacts, and weather vanes.

DON BADERTSCHER IMPORTS
716 North La Cienega
   Boulevard
Los Angeles, CA 90069
(213) 655-6448
Dressers, fireplaces, garden furniture, kitchen accessories, overmantels, and sideboards, mostly late nineteenth and early twentieth century, many imported from Europe.

BALASSES HOUSE ANTIQUES
Main Street
Amagansett, NY 11930
(516) 267-3032
Pine farm tables, corner cupboards, sideboards, Windsor chairs, brass lamps, antique kitchenware, and hanging light fixtures.

BRITISH COUNTRY ANTIQUES
Route 6
Woodbury, CT 06798
Polished pine country furniture from England or the Continent; unusual early paint-decorated armoires; large collection of country accessories.

BULL AND BEAR ANTIQUES
1189 Howell Mill Road, N.W.
Atlanta, GA 30318
(404) 355-6697
Eighteenth-century furniture; Staffordshire figures.

RICHARD CAMP
Montauk Highway
Wainscott, NY, 11975
(516) 537-0330
Bamboo and pine furniture, platters, bowls, and country antiques.

CHARTERHOUSE ANTIQUES
   LTD.
115 Greenwich Avenue
New York, NY 10014
(212) 243-4726
Small pieces of antique furniture, mostly English; also porcelain, pottery, decanters, rummers, and silver objects.

COUNTRY ACCENTS
Country Walk Shops
Highway 42
Sister Bay, WI 54234
(414) 854-4790
Antiques, Americana, silver, and country furniture.

THE COUNTRY SAMPLER
127 East Main Street
Fredericksburg, TX 78624
(512) 997-9620
Country accessories, gifts, and reproductions of antiques.

CROFT ANTIQUES
11 South Main Street
Southampton, NY 11968
(516) 283-6445
Antique country furniture and artifacts.

ENGLISH HERITAGE
8424 Melrose Place
Los Angeles, CA 90069
(213) 655-5946
Country and formal furniture and fine Georgian silver.

EVERGREEN ANTIQUES
1249 Third Avenue
New York, NY 10021
(212) 744-5664

120 Spring Street
New York, NY 10012
(212) 966-6458
Scandinavian country antiques and accessories.

MALCOME FRANKLIN, INC.
15 East 57th Street
New York, NY 10022
(212) 308-3344

126 East Delaware Place
Chicago, IL 60611
(312) 337-0202
Fine eighteenth-century furniture and accessories including clocks and mirrors.

PATTY GARGARIN
975 Banks North Road
Fairfield, CT 06430
(203) 259-7332
Early American antiques and folk art, specializing in fine painted furniture.

FRANCIS GIBBONS
1119 South La Brea Avenue
Los Angeles, CA 90019
(213) 937-0452
Country furniture, accessories, and gifts.

HARRY B. HARTMAN
Marietta, PA 17547
By appointment only
(717) 426-1474
Pennsylvania antiques and folk art.

HARRY B. HARTMAN
INTERIOR DESIGNS
Marietta, PA 17547
By appointment only
(717) 426-1474
Interior design and restoration.

JACKSON-MITCHELL, INC.
412 Delaware Street
New Castle, DE 19720
(303) 322-4363
Formal and country antique furniture and artifacts including brass, copper, and decorative metalware.

JAMES II GALLERIES, INC.
15 East 57th Street
New York, NY 10022
(212) 355-7040
Antique candlesticks, glass, ivory, miniatures, papier-mâché, pillboxes, picture frames, porcelain, pottery, silver and silverplate; small pieces of antique furniture including bamboo pieces, hat stands, and chairs.

JENKINTOWN ANTIQUES
520 Route 32 South
New Paltz, NY 12561
(914) 255-8135
American antiques and folk art, specializing in Hudson

River artifacts and furniture. Decorating service also.

HOWARD KAPLAN ANTIQUES
827 Broadway
New York, NY 10003
(212) 674-1000
French and English country antiques and furnishings.

MRS. BETTY MANNON
Highway 18 South
Boliver, TN 38995
(901) 658-9440
Simple Tennessee plantation furniture from the nineteenth century to the 1930s.

J. GARVIN MECKING, INC.
72 East 11th Street
New York, NY 10003
(212) 677-4316
Primarily nineteenth-century furniture and decorative accessories including antique needlepoint, bamboo and twig furniture, lacquerware, majolica, papier-mâché, objects with animal motifs, tole, decorative folk art, and painted country furniture.

MILL HOUSE ANTIQUES
Route 6
Woodbury, CT 06798
(203) 263-3446
Antique walnut, pine, and mahogany furniture, Welsh dressers, hunt boards, and desks.

ANN MORRIS ANTIQUES
239 East 60th Street
New York, NY 10022
(212) 755-3308
Formal and country antique furniture; billiard lights, various lighting fixtures including eighteenth- and nineteenth-century chandeliers; vitrines, large cabinets, shop cases, tables, kitchen crockery, and more.

PIPKA'S
322 Mill Road
Sister Bay, WI 54234
(414) 854-4392
Apenländische Volkskunst—Old World arts and crafts from Austria, Bavaria, and Switzerland; specializing in Bauernmalerei—German folk art painting, painted furniture.

RALF'S ANTIQUES
807 North La Cienega
Boulevard
Los Angeles, CA 90069
(213) 659-1966
Seventeenth-, eighteenth-, and nineteenth-century country furniture, copper and brass accessories, bronze figurines, and pictures.

THE SETTLERS' HOUSE
329 East Main Street
Fredericksburg, TX 78624
(512) 997-9621
Reproduction folk art furniture and antiques.

THE SWEDISH COTTAGE
1281 Madison Avenue
New York, NY 10128
(212) 534-8438
Swedish painted country furniture, turn-of-the-century frames, kerosene lamps, and porcelain.

THE WICKER GARDEN
1318 Madison Avenue
New York, NY 10128
(212) 410-7000
Large selection of wicker furniture, including Victorian and Art Deco; also brass and iron beds and accessories.

WINSOR ANTIQUES
53 Sherman Street
Fairfield, CT 06430
(203) 255-0056

Country furniture from late seventeenth century to Victorian, including stripped pine, French Provincial fruitwood, Georgian, and English oak; also decorative antiques, early ironware, prints, baskets, American decoys; specializes in English Windsor and ladderback chairs.

THOMAS K. WOODARD
835 Madison Avenue
New York, NY 10021
(212) 988-2906
American antiques, quilts, rag runners; accessories including baskets and pottery. Custom rugs made to specifications.

COUNTRY CRAFTS:

Baskets, Chair Bottoming, Dolls, Framing, Glasswork, Metalwork, Pottery, Quilting and Smocking, Sign Making, Sporting Goods, and Woodwork

JEWEL ALLEN
Whiteville, TN 38075
Chair bottoms made from twisted corn shucks in several different weaves; also cornhusk brooms.

MARTHA JEWELL ANDERSON
401 Jefferson Street
Boliver, TN 38008
Custom-made stained glass using Tennessee motifs such as bales of cotton, quail, and ducks.

ARCHITECTURAL PANELING,
INC.
979 Third Avenue
New York, NY 10022
(212) 371-9632
*Hand-carved mantels,
fireplaces, wood paneling and
moldings; woodwork made to
order.*

ARTISTIC BRASS
4100 Ardmore Avenue
South Gate, CA 90280
(213) 564-1100
*Brass bathroom hardware with
porcelain, wood, chrome,
crystal, malachite, marble,
rose quartz, tigereye, 24-carat
gold, and Wedgwood detailing.*

BLUEMLE–VON KOFFLER
STUDIO AND WORKSHOP
8499 Highway 42
Fish Creek, WI 54212
(414) 868-2020
*Stained, kiln-fired and
slumped, sandblasted, and
carved glass sculptural pieces,
wall murals and mosaics,
room dividers, tables, and
entrance halls.*

CLAY BAY POTTERY
Highway 42 and Old Stage Road
Ellison Bay, WI 54210
(414) 854-5027
*Artist-designed tiles, lamps,
and vases.*

COLE'S TOLE AND COUNTRY
Fish Creek, WI 54212
(414) 868-3929
*Unfinished woodenware made
especially for the rosemaler
and country painter; also art
supplies, patterns, and finished
pieces.*

THE CUSTOM WOOD
COMPANY
Highway 42
Egg Harbor, WI 54209
(414) 868-3932

*Deep-routed and raised-letter
signs, plus custom-made
furniture and repairs.*

*THE DECORATIVE
HARDWARE STUDIO
180 Hunts Lane
Chappaqua, NY 10514
(914) 238-5220
*Showrooms in Chicago, Dallas,
Houston, and New Orleans.
Importers and fabricators of
specialty and custom
hardware, including brass and
porcelain bathroom taps,
locks, knobs, kickplates,
pushplates, closet rods,
handrails, and cabinet
hardware. Brass carpet rods
available exclusively through
fine carpet showrooms
nationwide; draperies sold
through decorative fabric
houses nationwide. Call for
information and
comprehensive catalog.*

DUNN'S
Grand Junction, TN 38039
(800) 223-8667
(901) 784-2193
*Sporting clothes, field trial
equipment, Jaeger fine guns.
Sporting museum at back of
store.*

EDGEWOOD ORCHARD
GALLERY
Peninsula Players Road
Fish Creek, WI 54212
(414) 868-3579
*Architecturally designed hand-
built furniture, leaded and
etched glass windows; also
exhibitions showing artist-
designed ceramics, fiber, glass,
jewelry, metal, paintings,
prints, and woodwork.*

THE EIGHT OF PENTACLES
Walkway Mall, Highway 42
Sister Bay, WI 54234
(414) 854-4825

*Glass lamps, panels, sun
catchers, using fusing,
painting, sandblasting, and
etching techniques; also
repairs; frames and furniture
made of weathered wood.*

EK TRÄDET
Highway 57
Bailey's Harbor, WI 54202
(414) 839-2154
*"Wearable art," handwoven
products, craft materials,
baskets, rugs. Classes offered
in weaving, felting, basketry,
and many other crafts. Large
selection of fibers and looms.*

GREAT AMERICAN SALVAGE
CO.
34 Cooper Square
New York, NY 10003
(212) 505-0070

P.O. Box 509
Sag Harbor, NY 11963
(516) 725-2272

97 Crown Street
New Haven, CT 06508
(203) 624-1009

3 Main Street
Montpelier, VT 05602
(802) 223-7711

1630 Jacksonville, FL 32207
(904) 396-8081

*Antique architectural building
artifacts including stained
glass, doors, mantels, columns,
lighting fixtures, pedestal
sinks, bars, and bathroom
fixtures.*

HARTMANN GALLERY & SIGN
STUDIO
County Road ZZ at Sumac Lane
Sister Bay, WI 54234
(414) 854-5378

*Hand-lettered signs on panels,
trucks, windows; routed and
carved wood signs, engravings
on desks or wall plaques, and
hex signs.*

THE HEARTHSTONE
2711 East Coast Highway
Corona del Mar, CA 92625
(714) 673-7065
*Fireplace tools, grates, and
accessories in brass, steel, and
chrome; antique fenders,
custom-made door screens,
antique fireplace fixtures, jamb
hooks, trivets, trammel hooks,
hobs, and andirons.*

HORTON BRASSES
P.O. Box 95, Nooks Hill Road
Cromwell, CT 06416
(203) 635-4400
*Brass cabinet reproduction
hardware in Hepplewhite,
Sheraton, Queen Anne,
Chippendale, and Victorian
styles.*

IRONWOOD STUDIO AND
GALLERY
County Trunk A and
Junction Road
Jacksonport, WI 54202
(414) 823-2418
*Iron accessories for kitchens,
bathrooms, fireplaces; custom-
made ironwork; wood
furniture.*

THE MITRED TOUCH FLOWER
AND FRAME SHOP
19 Green Bay Road
Sturgeon Bay, WI 54235
(414) 743-3331
*Acid-free conservation framing
for fine artwork, custom-made
mats—straight, ovals, circles,
single or multiple openings,
layered mats. Also handwoven
rugs and flowers.*

PUTNAM ROLLING LADDER
   CO.
32 Howard Street
New York, NY 10013
(212) 226-5147
*Rolling library ladders in oak
made to order.*

ARTHUR SAGEBIEL
610 East San Antonio Street
Fredericksburg, TX 78624
(512) 997-9035
*Contractor, building restorer;
also creates folk art pieces in
wood and stone.*

JUDY VON SHACKEFORD
320 Union Street
Boliver, TN 38008
(901) 658-3877
*Hand smocking on collars and
yokes.*

MRS. CLINT H. SITES
Hornsby Road
Boliver, TN 38008
(901) 658-2325
*Dolls with faces made from
apples and fabric bodies; also
china dolls.*

ENLOE SMITH
Park Swain Road
Grand Junction, TN 38039
(901) 764-2054
*Baskets of many varieties
including cotton baskets made
of split-oak saplings. These are
three feet wide and four feet
tall and are used for gathering
cotton.*

SOLEBURY FORGE
937 Panns Park Road
P.O. Box 130
Wycombe, PA 18980
(215) 598-3336
*Custom-made ironwork; work
of any size in various metals.*

MRS. KENNETH STEVENS
117 Tennessee Street
Boliver, TN 38008
(901) 658-3361
*Handworked quilting,
needlepoint, and smocking.*

PATRICIA STEVENS
Clift Road
Boliver, TN 38008
(901) 658-4767
*Street-sign lettering; also
repairs on antique carpets and
tapestries.*

TENNESSEE PEWTER
Madison Avenue
Grand Junction, TN 38039
(901) 764-2091
*Pewter candlesticks, platters,
cups, quail and fox pins.*

RUTH WOLFGRAM
By appointment only
Old Stage Road
Ephraim, WI 54211
(414) 854-4611
*Traditional Norwegian
rosemaling and folk art.*

THE WRECKING BAR, INC.
2601 McKinney
Dallas, TX 75204
(214) 826-1717
*Architectural paneling, doors,
mantels, stairways, fire grates,
lighting fixtures.*

VETERANS' CANING
550 West 35th Street
New York, NY 10001
(212) 868-3244
*Hand and machine caning,
rush work, splint work, and
repair work.*

YORKVILLE CANING
31-04 60th Street
Woodside, NY 11377
(718) 274-6464

*Handworked and machine-
made caning, rush seating,
Shaker chairs; hand-woven
Danish wicker seats.*

DECORATION

*Including Fabrics,
Household Linens, Floor
and Wall Coverings, and
Paint Work*

AD HOC SOFTWARES
410 West Broadway
New York, NY 10012
(212) 925-2652
*Cotton flannel sheets, bed
linens, woolen blankets,
mohair throws, rag rugs, bath
mats and towels, soaps,
kitchen linens, and lace
curtains.*

LAURA ASHLEY
More than 86 stores across the
country and more planned; for
information call (800)
223-6917.
In addition, there is a full
decorator service in Boston,
New York, and San Francisco
and an interior design
consultant service in Chicago,
Dallas, and Los Angeles.
The Laura Ashley Decorator
Collection* of fabrics and wall
coverings is a special group
available only through
architects and decorators.
*Upholstery fabrics including
chintz, dobby weaves, union-
dyed linen/cotton, country
furnishing cotton prints, with
coordinated wall coverings
including borders; accessories,
lamps, lamp shades, cushions,
upholstered furniture, tiles,
paint, tiebacks, fringes, braids,
all in coordinating colors; bed
linens, shams, comforters,
made-to-measure curtains and
blinds.*

*DORIS LESLIE BLAU
   GALLERY, INC.
15 East 57th Street
New York, NY 10022
(212) 759-3715
*Exemplary and decorative
antique carpets and tapestries.*

*BOUSSAC
979 Third Avenue
New York, NY 10022
(212) 421-0534
*16 stores throughout the
country.
Large selection of decorative
fabrics and coordinating
wallpapers, including French
country prints.*

BRADBURY & BRADBURY
   WALLPAPERS
P.O. Box 155
Benicia, CA 94510
(707) 746-1900
*Silk-screened wallpapers and
borders of varied sizes in
documentary Victorian and
William Morris style designs.
Design service also available.*

*BRUNSCHWIG & FILS, INC.
979 Third Avenue
New York, NY 10022
(212) 838-7878
*Showrooms also in Atlanta,
Chicago, Dallas, Los Angeles,
Miami and Washington, D.C.
Also available at E. Wells
McLean, Boston; Regency Hour,
Denver and San Francisco;
Ellouise Abbot Showroom,
Houston; A.F. Brown,
Philadelphia; Designer
Showroom, Seattle; and E.D.
Navarra, Troy, Michigan.
Large selection of many
varieties of furnishing fabrics
and wall coverings, many from
documentary designs.*

CHERCHEZ
862 Lexington Avenue
New York, NY 10021
(212) 737-8215

Antique table and bed linens, paisley throws, needlepoint cushions and samplers.

*CLARENCE HOUSE
211 East 58th Street
New York, NY 10022
(212) 752-2890
Showrooms also in Atlanta, Boston, Chicago, Dallas, Denver, Houston, Los Angeles, Miami, Philadelphia, Portland, and San Francisco.
Fabrics, wallpapers, and trimmings; hand-blocked document chintzes including the Colefax & Fowler English prints; striéd, spattered, and grained wallpapers and borders, and leather.

CONRAN'S
160 East 54th Street
New York, NY 10022
(212) 371-2225
Stores also in Fairfax, VA; Georgetown, Washington, D.C.; New Haven, CT; Hackensack and Cherry Hills, NJ; King of Prussia, PA; Manhasset and New Rochelle, NY; Willow Grove, PA; Bethesda, MD; and Boston, MA.
Mail order only:
4 South Middlesex Avenue
Cranbury, NJ 08512
(609) 655-4505
Furnishing fabrics and coordinated wall coverings; sheets, duvet covers, and table linens; dhurrie rugs and oversized pillows; large range of contemporary furniture and kitchen systems.

COUNTRY CURTAINS
At the Red Lion Inn, Dept. 1087
Stockbridge, MA 01262
(413) 243-9910
Curtains in cotton, muslin, and carefree permanent press; bed ensembles.

*COWTAN & TOUT
979 Third Avenue
New York, NY 10022
(212) 753-4488
Available also at Travis & Company, Atlanta; Devon Service, Boston; Rozmallin, Chicago and Troy, MI; John Edward Hughes, Dallas and Houston; Denver, Los Angeles, San Francisco, Seattle, and Philadelphia.
Chintzes in florals, stripes, and striés with coordinating wall coverings; hand-blocked document designs; paisleys printed on wool, cotton, silk, and linen.

CREATIVE FINISHES
216 East 6th Street
New York, NY 10003
(212) 420-1813
Decorative paint work including trompe l'oeil, faux bois, *stencils, glazes, and marbleizing.*

*ROSE CUMMING CHINTZ, LTD.
232 East 59th Street
New York, NY 10022
(212) 758-0844
Showrooms also in Atlanta, Boston, Chicago, Dallas, Houston, Los Angeles, San Francisco, and Washington, D.C.
Documentary chintzes. Rose Cumming, Inc. sells antique furniture and accessories to the trade at the same New York showroom.

*DECORATORS' WALK
245 Newtown Road
Plainview, NY 11803
(516) 249-3100
Represents many companies with a variety of fabrics, wallpapers, casements, sheers, textures, damasks, prints, chintzes, stripes, checks, dots, velvets, satins, taffetas.

*EAGLESHAM PRINTS, INC.
979 Third Avenue
New York, NY 10022
(212) 759-2060
Custom hand-printed patterns of various furnishing fabrics, with coordinating wall coverings.

*FONTHILL
979 Third Avenue
New York, NY 10022
(212) 924-3000
Marbleized and striéd chintzes and wallpapers; hand-blocked documentary designed chintzes.

*PHILIP GRAF WALLPAPERS, INC.
979 Third Avenue
New York, NY 10022
(212) 755-1448
Country-style wallpapers with coordinating fabrics available. Other fabrics include grasscloth, prints, stripes, dots, textures, mostly traditional in feeling.

*GREEFF FABRICS, INC.
155 East 56th Street
New York, NY 10022
(212) 824-6200
Traditional prints and textures.

*HINSON & CO.
979 Third Avenue
New York, NY 10022
(212) 475-4100
Country-style wallpapers and fabrics. The Hinson Collection is a licensee of the Metropolitan Museum of Art, The American Wing. Collections of wallpapers and fabrics available through interior designers and fine stores throughout the country.

JEAN HOFFMAN–JANA STARR ANTIQUES
236 East 80th Street
New York, NY 10021
(212) 535-6930
Antique bed and table linens and laces, pillows, lace panels, and lace curtains.

*JONES & ERWIN, INC.
515 Andrews Road
Trevose, PA 19047
(800) 523-5256
Country-style wallpapers in traditional and contemporary prints. Can do custom coloring.

*KATZENBACH & WARREN, INC.
979 Third Avenue
New York, NY 10022
(212) 759-5416
Authentic reproductions of documentary wallpapers including four Williamsburg collections and three Waterhouse collections.

RALPH LAUREN HOME COLLECTION
Shops in fine department stores and selected Polo/Ralph Lauren shops throughout the country. Call for up-to-date listing: (212) 930-3200
Solid and striped oxford cotton bedding; sheets and pillowcases in soft florals, tattersall checks, plaids, and paisleys, all with coordinating bedspreads, throws, shams, and bed skirts; towels, shower curtains, and bath mats; table linens, place mats, and napkins; brass bath accessories, wall coverings, fabric by the yard, floor coverings, pillows, and upholstered furniture; wicker and rattan.

*LEE-JOFA, INC.
979 Third Avenue
New York, NY 10022
(212) 688-0444
Showrooms also in Atlanta, Boston, Chicago, Dallas, Los Angeles, Philadelphia, San Francisco, and Washington, D.C.
Cotton and linen prints, hand-blocked chintzes, damasks, horsehairs, laces, and wall coverings; marbleized wallpapers and chintzes; trimmings.

LIBERTY OF LONDON SHOPS, INC.
3222 M Street, NW
Georgetown Park No. 249
Washington, D.C. 20007
(202) 388-3711
Shops also in New York, Ardmore, PA, and Chicago. Liberty floral prints of fine Tana lawn, highly glazed chintzes in traditional designs, William Morris and Art Nouveau designs, sheets and duvet covers (through Martex, Inc.), picture frames and gift objects.

*JOSEPH MELLAND
32 Union Square
New York, NY 10003
(212) 995-9352
Floorcloths painted using traditional techniques; fancy paint brushes of all kinds, including faux bois, faux marbre, porphyry, stencils, glazes, and trompe l'oeil.

ELINOR MERRELL
By appointment only
New York, NY
(212) 288-4986
Antique European fabrics.

MOTIF DESIGN
90 Lyncroft Road
New Rochelle, NY 10804
(914) 636-7973

Decorator service specializing in kitchens and bathrooms; exclusively designed fabric by the yard.

MICHAEL TYSON MURPHY STUDIO
346 West 56th Street
New York, NY 10019
(212) 502-0178
Decorative paint work including trompe l'oeil, murals, faux bois, glazes, and stencils.

FRANÇOISE NUNNALLE
By appointment only
New York, NY
(212) 246-4281
Antique linens and lace; large selection of decorative antique tiebacks.

ELLEN O'NEILL SUPPLY STORE
242 East 77th Street
New York, NY 10028
Antique linens, quilts, Marseilles cloth bedspreads, blankets, and fabrics.

PIERRE DEUX FABRICS
350 Bleecker Street
New York, NY 10014
(212) 741-7245
Mail order department: 147 Palmer Avenue Mamaroneck, NY 10543 (800) 8-PIERRE. In New York State call (800) 992-2998 or (914) 698-0555. Boutiques in Atlanta, Beverly Hills, Boston, Carmel, CA; Chicago, Dallas, Houston, Kansas City, New Orleans, New York, Palm Beach, San Francisco, Scottsdale, AZ; Seattle, Newport Beach, CA; and Washington, D.C. French country printed cottons, toile de Jouy; faience, pewter, glassware, floor tiles, and other accessories.

*SCALAMANDRE
950 Third Avenue
New York, NY 10022
(212) 980-3888
Showrooms also in Atlanta, Boston, Chicago, Dallas, Houston, Los Angeles, Miami, Philadelphia, San Francisco, and Washington, D.C., and representatives in other cities. Velvets, silks, damasks, printed cottons, and wall coverings; documentary William Morris designs; trimming and carpets.

TOPALIAN TRADING COMPANY
281 Fifth Avenue
New York, NY 10016
(212) 684-0735
Antique Oriental carpets.

THE VERMONT COUNTRY STORE
P.O. Box 3000
Manchester Center, VT 055255-3000
(802) 362-2400
Traditional cotton yard goods including ticking, batiste, and toweling.

*WAVERLY, A DIVISION OF F. SCHUMACHER & CO.
Call (212) 704-9900 for locations.
Traditional country prints and patterns from Victorian styles to the 1930s and 1940s.

PUBLICATIONS

Agriculture and Animals

THE BACKSTRETCH
United Thoroughbred Trainers of America, Inc.
19363 James Couzens Highway
Detroit, MI 48235
(313) 342-6144

For thoroughbred horse trainers, owners, breeders, farm managers, track personnel, jockeys, grooms, and racing fans.

CALIFORNIA GROWER
Rancher Publications
P.O. Box 2047
Vista, CA 92083
(619) 744-7170
Monthly industrial and consumer magazine about avocado, citrus, and subtropical fruit growing.

COUNTRYSIDE AND SMALL STOCK JOURNAL
312 Highway 19 East
Waterloo, WI 53594
(414) 478-2115
Monthly magazine about practical small farming, homesteading, and organic agriculture.

FARM JOURNAL
230 West Washington Square
Philadelphia, PA 19106
(215) 829-4700
Published 11 times a year; covers all aspects of small and commercial farming.

HORSEMAN'S JOURNAL
2800 Grand Route St. John
New Orleans, LA 70119
(504) 948-4848
Monthly magazine for thoroughbred racehorse owners, breeders, officials, and fans.

HORSEMAN'S YANKEE PEDLAR NEWSPAPER
785 South Bridge Street
Auburn, MA 01501
(617) 832-9638
The Northeast's largest equine monthly publication.

ORGANIC GARDENING AND
   FARMING
Rodale Press Inc.
33 East Minor Street
Emmaus, PA 18049
(215) 967-5171
*Monthly magazine devoted to
backyard gardening and
family farming using organic
methods.*

THE WESTERN HORSEMAN
P.O. Box 7980
Colorado Springs, CO 80933
(303) 633-5524
*50-year-old monthly magazine
about horse training, rodeos,
ranch life, and history relating
to the Western horse.*

THE WINE SPECTATOR
M. Shanken Communications,
   Inc.
Opera Plaza Suite 2040
601 Van Ness Avenue
San Francisco, CA 94102
(415) 673-2040
*Bi-monthly magazine about
vineyards and wine.*

Antiques

THE ANTIQUARIAN
P.O. Box 798
Huntington Station, NY 11743
(516) 271-8990
*Monthly magazine containing
historical articles on
eighteenth- to nineteenth-
century antiques and
furnishings.*

ANTIQUES AND THE ARTS
   WEEKLY
The Bee Publishing Co.
5 Church Hill Road
Newtown, CT 06470
(203) 426-3141
*Weekly newspaper with
articles on antiques, auctions,
shows, and fairs.*

JOEL SATER'S ANTIQUES AND
   AUCTION NEWS
P.O. Box 500
Route 230
West Mount Joy, PA 17552
(717) 653-9797
*Weekly newspaper for
antiquers and collectors with
historical articles, interviews,
and articles on how to restore
or preserve antiques.*

MAINE ANTIQUE DIGEST
P.O. Box 645
Waldoboro, ME 04572
(207) 832-7534
*Monthly publication about
early Americana, antique
furniture, marine artifacts,
redware, folk art, and Shaker
products.*

ANTIQUE REVIEW
P.O. Box 538
Worthington, OH 43085
(614) 885-9757
*Monthly publication about the
history, production, and
current market values of
furniture pottery, china, and
other arts and crafts, with an
emphasis on items more than
100 years old.*

ANTIQUE WEEK
P.O. Box 90
Knightstown, IN 46148
(317) 345-5134
*Weekly newspaper printed in
two separate editions, Mid
Central and Mid Atlantic, with
articles on antiques,
collectibles, history, genealogy,
and restorations.*

ART AND ANTIQUES
89 Fifth Avenue
New York, NY 10003
(212) 206-7050

*Published 10 times a year,
focusing on both the fine and
decorative arts. Contains
articles about current shows
and listings of gallery and
museum openings.*

ART AND AUCTION
250 West 57th Street
New York, NY 10019
(212) 582-5633
*Monthly magazine about
houses, antiques, collectors,
and galleries.*

HISTORIC PRESERVATION
1785 Massachusetts Avenue,
   N.W.
Washington, D.C. 20036
(202) 673-4000
*Magazine for members of the
National Trust; encourages
public participation in the
preservation of sites, buildings,
and objects significant in
American history and culture.*

THE OLD BOTTLE MAGAZINE
Maverick Publications
Drawer 5007
Bend, OR 97708
(503) 382-6978
*Monthly publication with
stories about relics of the
industrial age.*

Design and Decorating

ARCHITECTURAL DIGEST
Knapp Communications
Corporation
5900 Wilshire Boulevard
Los Angeles, CA 90036
(213) 937-4740
*Glossy monthly magazine
about international haute
decoration.*

BETTER HOMES AND
   GARDENS
1716 Locust Street
Des Moines, IA 50336
(515) 284-3000
*Monthly magazine devoted to
decorating and building, food,
health, education, and general
family issues.*

COLONIAL HOMES
1790 Broadway
New York, NY 10019
(212) 830-2900
*Interiors and exteriors of
colonial houses in America and
abroad.*

COUNTRY LIVING
224 West 57th Street
New York, NY 10019
(212) 262-5626
*Monthly magazine about
decorating, crafts, cooking,
real estate, and antiques.*

HOUSE AND GARDEN
The Condé Nast Building
350 Madison Avenue
New York, NY 10017
(212) 880-8800
*Glossy monthly magazine
showing mostly grand
interiors. There is a completely
different British* House and
Garden *and a French version,*
Maison et Jardin.

HOUSE BEAUTIFUL
1700 Broadway
New York, NY 10019
(212) 903-5100
*Monthly magazine featuring
decorating, design,
architecture, food,
entertaining, and furniture.*

NEW YORK TIMES MAGAZINE
   SECTION
229 West 43rd Street
New York, NY 10036
(212) 556-7369

Weekly magazine supplement to the Sunday New York Times; *decorating features of all varieties.*

THE WORLD OF INTERIORS
234 Kings Road
London SW3 5UA, England
Glossy magazine about superior decorating, whether in the city or the country.

General Interest

COUNTRY LIVING
224 West 57th Street
New York, NY 10019
(212) 262-5656
Monthly magazine about decorating, crafts, cooking, real estate, and antiques.

MOTHER EARTH NEWS
80 Fifth Avenue
17th Floor
New York, NY 10011
(212) 645-2661
Complete lifestyle magazine, published bi-monthly, for country living.

PRACTICAL HOME OWNER
708 Third Avenue
New York, NY 10017
(212) 697-2040
Monthly magazine containing articles on home improvement, remodeling, and building new homes.

TOWN AND COUNTRY
1700 Broadway
New York, NY 10019
(212) 903-5000
Monthly international magazine about houses, decorating, and personalities.

Regional Magazines

HUDSON VALLEY MAGAZINE
Suburban Publishing Inc.
P.O. Box 429
Poughkeepsie, NY 12602
(914) 485-7844
Monthly magazine with articles on regional entertainment and leisure.

NEW ENGLAND MONTHLY
Box 446
Haydenville, MA 01039
(413) 268-7262
Monthly magazine with offbeat New England articles on travel, leisure, and the arts.

NORTHERN VIRGINIA
P.O. Box 1177
Vienna, VA 22180
(703) 938-0666
Bi-monthly magazine featuring both current and historical articles about the people and places of northern Virginia.

REFLEXIONS
The White Pond Center
P.O. Box 800, White Pond Road
Stormville, NY 12582
(914) 878-9114
Tri-annual magazine of cultural, historical, and local interest serving Putnam and Dutchess Counties in New York State.

SOUTHERN ACCENTS
Southern Accents, Inc.
1718 Peachtree Road, N.W.
Suite 1080 South
Atlanta, GA 30359
(404) 874-4462
Bi-monthly magazine featuring fine Southern homes and gardens.

YANKEE
Main Street
Dublin, NH 03444
(603) 563-8111
Monthly magazine about New England, its arts and crafts, fiction, poetry, personalities, reminiscences, nature, and antiques.

YANKEE MAGAZINE'S TRAVEL
   GUIDE TO NEW ENGLAND
Main Street
Dublin, NH 03444
Published annually, in the spring, this guide gives information on where to go, what to do, and where to stay in New England, New York, and Canada.

BIBLIOGRAPHY

BOOKS

Arthur, Eric and Whitney, Dudley. *The Barn: A Vanishing Landmark in North America.* Greenwich, Conn.: New York Graphic Society, 1972.

Bacon, Margaret Hope. *The Quiet Rebels: The Story of the Quakers in America.* Philadelphia: New Society Publishers, 1985.

Benson, E.F. *As We Are: A Modern Review.* London: Longmans, Green & Co., 1932.

Bracken, Dorothy Kendall and Redway, Maurine Whorton. *Early Texas Homes.* Dallas: Southern Methodist University Press, 1956.

Dixon-Hunt, John and Willis, Peter. *The Genius of the Place: The English Landscape Garden 1620–1820.* London: Paul Elek, 1975.

Downing, Andrew Jackson. *The Architecture of Country Houses.* New York: Da Capo Press, 1968. Originally published, 1850.

Fitch, Marston. *American Building: The Historical Forces That Shaped It.* Boston: Houghton Mifflin Co., 1947, 1966.

Flatau, Richard. *Cordwood Construction: A Log End View.* Merrill, Wis.: Cordwood Publications, 1984.

Gidney, C.M.; Brooks, Benjamin; and Sheridan, Edwin M. *A History of Santa Barbara, San Luis Obispo and Ventura Counties, California.* Vol. II. Chicago: Lewis Publishing Co., 1917.

Handlin, David P. *The American Home: Architecture and Society 1815–1915.* Boston: Little, Brown and Co., 1979.

Hasbrouck, Kenneth E. *The Street of the Huguenots.* New York: Charles E. Tuttle Co. First published, Goshen, N.Y.: The Bookmill on Windy Hill, 1952.

Hatch, Alden. *The Byrds of Virginia: An American Dynasty, 1670 to the Present.* New York: Holt, Rinehart & Winston, 1969.

Hubka, Thomas C. *Big House, Little House, Back House, Barn: The Connected Farm Buildings of New England.* Hanover, N.H.: University Press of New England, 1984.

Josephy, Alvin M., Jr., ed. *The American Heritage Book of Indians.* New York: American Heritage Publishing Company, 1961.

Kahlert, John. *Early Door County Buildings (and the People Who Built Them 1849–1910).* 2nd ed. Bailey's Harbor, Wis.: Meadow Lane Publishers, 1978.

Kauffman, Henry J. *The American Farmhouse: New England Down to Georgia and West to Ohio.* New York: Hawthorne, 1975.

Ketchum, William C., Jr. *Volume 2 of The Knopf Collectors' Guides to American Antiques: Furniture, Chests, Cupboards, Desks & Other Pieces.* New York: Alfred A. Knopf, 1982.

Kowert, Elise. *Historic Homes In And Around Fredericksburg.* Fredericksburg, Tex.: Fredericksburg Standard Radio Post.

Leatherman, Carroll Seabrook. *The Old Man . . . And the Dog.* Princeton, N.J.: Nassau Press, 1984.

Link, Mike. *Journeys to Door County.* Edina, Minn.: Voyageur Press, 1985.

McAlester, Virginia and Lee. *A Field Guide to American Houses.* New York: Alfred A. Knopf, 1984.

Monahan, Margaret B. *Richard Osborn: A Reminiscence.* Quaker Hill, N.Y.: Quaker Hill Conference Association, 1902.

Noble, Allen G. *Wood, Brick, & Stone: The North American Settlement Landscape.* Amherst: University of Massachusetts Press, 1984.

Nutting, Wallace. *A Furniture Treasury.* New York: Macmillan Co., 1948, 1954.

Overdyke, W. Darrell. *Louisiana Plantation Homes: Colonial and Antebellum.* New York: Crown Publishers, 1981.

Pearce, Nathaniel H. *Lights and Shadows of Pawling.* Pawling, N.Y.: Historical Society of Quaker Hill and Vicinity, 1934. Originally published, 1870.

Perrin, Richard W.E. *Historic Wisconsin Building: A Survey in Pioneer Architecture 1835–1870, 2nd ed.* Milwaukee: Milwaukee Public Museum, 1981.

Peterson, Harold L. *American Interiors: From Colonial Times to the Late Victorians.* New York: Charles Scribner's Sons, 1971.

Pratt, Dorothy and Richard. *A Guide to Early American Homes: North.* New York: McGraw-Hill Book Co., 1956.

Pratt, Dorothy and Richard. *A Guide to Early American Homes: South.* New York: McGraw-Hill Book Co., 1956.

Rawson, Richard. *Old Barn Plans.* New York: W H Smith Publishers, 1979.

Raymond, Eleanor. *Early Domestic Architecture of Pennsyvania.* Exton, Penn.: Shiffer, 1977.

Reynolds, Helen Wilkinson. *Dutch Houses in the Hudson Valley: Before 1776.* New York: Payon and Clarke, 1929.

Rouse, Parke, Jr. *Tidewater Virginia: In Color.* New York: Hastings House Publishers, 1968.

Rudofsky, Bernard. *Behind the Picture Window.* New York: Oxford University Press, 1955.

Rudofsky, Bernard. *Architecture Without Architects: An Introduction to Non-Pedigreed Architecture.* New York: Museum of Modern Art/Doubleday, 1969.

Rifkind, Carole. *A Field Guide to American Architecture.* New York: New American Library, 1980.

Schwartz, Marvin D. *Chairs, Tables, Sofas, Beds. Volume 1 of The Knopf Collectors' Guides to American Antiques.* New York: Alfred A. Knopf, 1982.

Scully, Vincent J., Jr. *The Shingle Style and The Stick Style: Architectural Theory and Design from Downing to the Origins of Wright.* Rev. ed. New Haven, Conn.: Yale University Press, 1971.

Shea, John G. *Antique Country Furniture of North America.* New York: Van Nostrand Reinholdt, 1975.

State Review Society of Historic Sites: 1964. Princeton, N.J.: D. Van Nostrand, 1964.

Stears, Amanda Akin. *Ancient Homes and Early Days of Quaker Hill.* Pawling, N.Y., 1903.

Stilgoe, John R. *Common Landscape of America: 1580 to 1845.* New Haven, Conn.: Yale University Press, 1982.

Taber, Alicia Hopkins. *Some Glimpses of the Past*. Quaker Hill, N.Y.: Quaker Hill Conference Association, 1905.

Taber, Martha A. *The Occupancy of Fredericksburgh*. Pawling, N.Y.: Akin Library, 1928.

Ulvilden, Pipka. *The Best of Door County, Wisconsin*. Sister Bay, Wis.: Pipka Publications, 1986.

Walker, Lester. *American Shelter: An Illustrated Encyclopedia of the American Home*. Woodstock, N.Y.: Overlook Press, 1981.

Whiffen, Marcus, and Koeper, Frederick. *American Architecture 1607–1976*. Cambridge, Mass.: MIT Press, 1981.

Wilson, Rev. Warren H. *Quaker Hill in the Eighteenth Century*. Quaker Hill, N.Y.: Quaker Hill Conference Association, 1901.

Woodall, Ronald, and Watkins, T.H. *Taken by the Wind: Vanishing Architecture of the West*. New York: Crown Publishers, 1981.

Worlidge, John. *Systeme Agricultura: The Mystery of HUSBANDRY Discovered*. Facsimile ed. Los Angeles: Sherwin & Freutel, 1970. Originally published, 1675.

Wright, Louis B. and Tinling, Marion, eds. *The Secret Diary of William Byrd of Westover: The Great American Gentleman: 1709–1712*. New York: G.P. Putnam's Sons, 1963.

PERIODICALS

Branston, John. "The Champions." *The Commercial Appeal Mid-South Magazine* (Memphis, Tenn.), March 17, 1985, pp. 4–10.

Ditmer, Joanne. "Life in a Log Cabin." *Empire Magazine, The Denver Post*, December 5, 1976, p. 60.

Drew, Bernard. "Shays Battle Re-Enactment in Feb. '87." *The Berkshire Courier* (Great Barrington, Mass.), January 23, 1986, p. 1.

Grund, Josephine. "'I can remember' . . . Conversations with the Zachow Sisters." *The Door County Advocate* (Sturgeon Bay, Wis.), September 4, 1979.

Laube, James. "Great Vineyards: René di Rosa of Winery Lake, One of California's First Growths." *The Wine Spectator* (San Francisco), December 1–15, 1985.

Lewis, Kim. "A Haven for the Mighty." *Mid-Atlantic Country Sun* (Alexandria, Va.), April, 1986, pp. 24–26.

Locke, Elizabeth. "At Home: Classic Clarke County." *Town & Country*, October 1985, pp. 238–248.

Lopez, Marie. "Ek Garden Workshop Part of House and Garden Walk." *The Door County Advocate* (Sturgeon Bay, Wis.), July 15, 1982, p. 6.

Olson, Lynne. "The Unlikely Creator of Hearst's San Simeon." *Smithsonian Magazine*, December 1985, pp. 60–71.

Paulsen, Alice. "A New Start in an Old Log Cabin." *Green Bay Press-Gazette*, October 14, 1979.

Perrin, Richard W.E. "Wisconsin's Stovewood Architecture." *Wisconsin Academy of Sciences, Arts and Letters*, Summer 1984.

Pinner, Cathy. "His Chairs Are Appearing in the Best Homes." *Bulletin-Times* (Tenn.), April 16, 1986, p. 6b.

Ray, Shirley G. "Wine and Art." *Wine Country* (San Francisco), February 1985, pp. 28–30, 56–57.

Reynolds, Henry. "Bird Dogs Point for Show." *The Commercial Appeal* (Memphis, Tenn.), December 13, 1985, p. c3.

"Sunday Houses Unique Reminders." *Fredericksburg Standard-Radio Post* (Fredericksburg, Tex.), March 26, 1986, p. 12.

"A Western Homestead." *Country Living*, May 1984, pp. 88–93.

"Zachow Reminiscences." *The Door County Advocate* (Sturgeon Bay, Wis.), September 4, 1979, sec. 1, p. 4.